Number

MATHS GAMES — KEY STAGE TWO

Joe Santaniello

Published by Scholastic Publications Ltd,
Villiers House, Clarendon Avenue,
Leamington Spa, Warwickshire CV32 5PR
© 1995 Scholastic Publications Ltd

AUTHOR Joe Santaniello
EDITOR Noel Pritchard
ASSISTANT EDITORS Joel Lane and Joanne Boden
SERIES DESIGNER Joy White
DESIGNER Toby Long
ILLUSTRATIONS Chris Saunderson
COVER ARTWORK Joy White

Designed using Aldus Pagemaker
Processed by Pages Bureau, Leamington Spa
Printed in Great Britain by Bell & Bain Ltd, Glasgow

British Library Cataloguing-in-Publication Data
A catalogue record for this book is available from the British Library.

ISBN 0-590-53359-2

Text © 1995 Joe Santaniello. The right of Joe Santaniello to be identified as the Author of this Work has been asserted by him in accordance with the Copyright, Designs and Patent Act 1988.

Material from the National Curriculum is Crown copyright and is reproduced by permission of the Controller of HMSO.

All rights reserved. This book is sold subject to the condition that it shall not, by way of trade or otherwise, be lent, hired out or otherwise circulated without the publisher's prior consent in any form of binding or cover other than that in which it is published and without a similar condition, including this condition, being imposed upon the subsequent purchaser.

No part of this publication may be reproduced, stored in a retrieval system, or transmitted, in any form or by any means, electronic, mechanical, photocopying, recording or otherwise, without the prior permission of the publisher. This book remains copyright, although permission is granted to copy pages on which the 'photocopiable' logo appears for classroom distribution and use only in the school which has purchased the book.

Contents

INTRODUCTION 5
The contribution of games to teaching
  and learning 6
Games and the Mathematics curriculum 7
The games 7
The teachers' notes 8
Assessment 8
Classroom management 9
Cross-curricular connections 9
Links to the National Curriculum 11
Links to the Scottish 5–14 Guidelines 12

ACTIVITY GAMES 13
Next in line 14
Make £1 15
Good guess! 16
Odds and evens 17
Criss cross 18
Make a multiple 20
Fizz! Buzz! 21
Four square 22
Name your number 23
What number am I? 24

PHOTOCOPIABLE GAMES 25
Eye spy a big number 26
At the cinema 29
Bags of numbers 33
Supermarket 37
Make a fiver 45
Coin hopscotch 48
Box office 52
City traffic 58
Square meal 62
What's the difference? 69
Noughty 73

Contents...

Skyline	77
100 squares or sequences	81
100 triangle diamonds	85
Carpet tiles	89
Palace in Numberland	93
Mt. Probability	98
Grand Prix	100
Super saver day	108
Number roulette	112
Choc shop	115
Number monorail	118
Remainders	123
Summit	126
Acrobats	129

SPECIAL SECTION — 133
Notes	134
Eye spy meter	138
Money meter	140
Decimal meter	142
Noughty meter	143
Number meter	144

COLOUR PULL-OUT GAMES
Summit
Acrobats

Introduction

INTRODUCTION

THE CONTRIBUTION OF GAMES TO TEACHING AND LEARNING

We live in a games-saturated culture. Outdoor sports and computer games are obvious examples at opposite ends of a spectrum that encompasses our everyday life. Games appeal to all sections of society, and are therefore levellers of difference. But games are often ephemeral. We play them. We forget them. Perhaps it is this transience which makes some teachers and parents sceptical of the value games have in learning. Games in school are often relegated to a peripheral role, as time-fillers or rewards for having completed 'important' work. The books in this series are an attempt to counterbalance this viewpoint by showing how games with clear learning objectives can be brought into the mainstream of primary teaching, to help develop key concepts and skills alongside any scheme of work.

In the context of mathematics teaching, games serve a number of educational purposes, providing an alternative forum for:
- using and applying mathematical skills and understanding;
- discussing mathematical concepts and developing mathematical language;
- developing the ability to follow instructions;
- developing co-operative learning, social and problem-solving skills;
- increasing motivation and subject interest;
- encouraging independence;
- bridging the gap between practical activities and more abstract methods of recording;
- assessing acquisition of skills and knowledge.

The games in this series of books also offer the following benefits. They:
- have clear educational objectives linked to the National Curriculum programmes of study and the Scottish 5-14 Guidelines;
- save time and money by providing photocopiable resources;
- can be adapted to suit individual needs and purposes;
- offer suggestions for differentiation;
- include game record sheets to promote data handling and record-keeping, and to provide evidence;
- have lively real-life and imaginary contexts to capture and hold the children's interest.

Number INTRODUCTION

GAMES AND THE MATHEMATICS CURRICULUM

All of these games have been devised to support Mathematics requirements in the National Curriculum and the Scottish 5–14 Guidelines. A vital element of many traditional games is the reinforcement of counting and number recognition skills. The games in this series build on these acknowledged benefits, extending them into less well-explored areas of the Mathematics curriculum within an atmosphere of pleasurable learning. The children's imagination is captured by interlacing the mathematical content with role-playing in both 'real' and fantasy worlds. The games provide a collaborative forum for discussion and, therefore, a focus for asking questions and developing mathematical language. The decision-making, prediction and reasoning skills outlined in Using and Applying Mathematics (Attainment Target 1) are developed in all the games, and the inclusion of game record sheets ensures that data handling is integrated throughout.

THE GAMES

This book contains both non-board based games (in the section called 'Activity games') as well as games that use boards and other manipulative resources (in the sections called 'Photocopiable games' and 'Special section').

ACTIVITY GAMES

This section provides a selection of ideas for games that only require resources commonly found in classrooms. Most of the games can be played by the whole class. Some are physical activity games and are best played in a large open space such as a hall, playground or field.

PHOTOCOPIABLE GAMES

The games in this section are based on photocopiable resources that are provided. These resources include game boards (some of which have a three-dimensional element), cards, game rules, game record sheets, and playing components such as spinners and playing pieces. These games follow traditional game formats and are designed to be played in small groups. The 'make-your-own' feature of the photocopiable sheets means that games can be adapted easily and without great expense.

When making the playing pieces, cut along solid lines and fold along dotted lines.

The following symbols are used on some of the photocopiable pages:

 A calculator may be useful.

 For construction, the sheet needs to be photocopied the number of times shown.

SPECIAL SECTION

This section contains photocopiable resources to be used with games from the photocopiable games section. They also have wider applications for other mathematics and cross-curricular activities.

THE TEACHERS' NOTES

The teachers' notes follow a standard format for each game:

TEACHING CONTENT

The mathematical learning objectives are signposted and linked to the National Curriculum programmes of study for Key Stage Two and the Scottish 5–14 Guidelines. For example: **(N: 3c; AS: C)** indicates National Curriculum Attainment Target **N**umber: Key Stage Two programme of study paragraph **3c**; Scottish 5–14 Guidelines for Number, Money and Measurement, strand **A**ddition and **S**ubtraction, Level **C**.

WHAT YOU NEED

Resources that you will need are listed under the following headings: 'Photocopiable sheets', 'For construction' and 'For playing'. It is recommended that where coins are needed, these be plastic or card play models.

PREPARATION

Notes are given on assembling the game and, where appropriate, suggestions made for introducing the game.

HOW TO PLAY

The aim and rules of the game are briefly summarised and any additional information for the teacher to consider is pointed out.

TEACHER'S ROLE

In some of the games the teacher is an active participant, in others a facilitator or an observer. This section helps the teacher to define her role and offers ideas for developing the game's mathematical ideas and skills. See also page 9.

GAME VARIATIONS

Where a game can be varied within the mathematical objectives set out under the 'Teaching content', ideas are given.

EXTENSION

Where a game might be extended to develop the mathematical objectives, ideas are given.

ASSESSMENT

There are three main ways that the teacher can assess the value of a game and the children's learning:

- Direct observation of the game in progress

Observation of a game allows the teacher to note how each child copes with the skills required in the game. A clipboard is handy for on-the-spot jotting down of notes. Be aware, however, that an adult presence can distort the game.

- Discussion after the game

After the game, the supervising adult can discuss what happened with

the group, extending the players' horizons beyond the 'who won' mentality. Where appropriate, pointers and suggested questions for doing this are given in the teachers' notes.

- Using game record sheets

Many games are accompanied by a game record sheet upon which the result and how it was achieved can be recorded by the players themselves, giving concrete evidence of how well they have assimilated the concept(s) behind the game. The game record sheets employ writing, drawing and data handling skills to give the busy teacher an outline of the completed game; in many cases, these sheets can be adapted to provide differentiation for the games.

CLASSROOM MANAGEMENT

As indicated above, not all the games are board games. There are card games, pencil and paper games, calculator games and mental games. This variety enables the teacher to select the appropriate game for the particular classroom situation, or even for sending home to be played with parents. Group games can be played at a table or in a designated corner. Some games are suitable for individual play – a copy of a single track, for instance, can be used both as a playing surface and as a record of the game – with the child competing against herself.

THE TEACHER'S ROLE

The teacher's main task will be in the selection of the game and the setting up of play for the designated educational purpose. She will need to decide what curricular function the game can serve. It can introduce a subject; it can reinforce skills or knowledge already touched on; or it can be a means of assessment. Most of the games and all the game sheets are ideal for assessment; suggestions for carrying this out are given, where appropriate, within the teachers' notes for each game.

Unless the children have played the game before, or are competent readers and can play well together on their own, the teacher (or another adult) will need to introduce and supervise the games. Ideas for introducing the games are given, where appropriate, in the teachers' notes to provide a context or stimulus for playing the game. Alternatively, the teacher can make up her own.

There is no sense in letting children play a game and then forget it. It needs to be followed up. In the teachers' notes for each game, there are suggestions about the part the supervising adult can play in enlarging the players' horizons beyond the actual playing of the game.

Obviously, the light of experience will indicate possible variations to the games, and the photocopiable pages enable the teacher to alter details and change rules to match individual needs and purposes.

MAKING AND STORING THE GAMES

Photocopiable games are flexible and inexpensive. Even elaborate board games can be made for pence, whereas comparable commercial games would cost pounds. Also, little more than the usual art materials found in most schools is needed for their construction. So instead of having just a few games to enhance motivation and learning, the teacher can afford to be quite lavish with them.

If possible, photocopy the game boards and playing pieces directly on to card.

The appearance and motivational benefit of the games can be greatly improved by colouring them in. Felt-tipped pens are best as they don't warp the paper as much as paint. Laminating the game boards and pieces also improves appearance and increases durability.

- Using parents and educational assistants

There is no reason why the teacher needs to do all the assembling. Games construction is a pleasurable activity involving colouring-in, cutting, pasting and, optionally, laminating. None of these tasks requires a teaching certificate! Parents, and even older pupils in the school, are quite capable of doing most of these things. Organise a games-making event involving both parents and pupils!

Similarly, a parent can be the games supervisor, instructing the group in the rules of the game, keeping an eye on its progress and conducting the discussion afterwards.

- Storing the games

Keep the various components of each game (e.g. board, pieces, game record sheets, 'How to play' sheets, and so on) in an individual strong polythene bag, fastened with a wire tie. These can be attached to a 'Mathematics games' board with a small bulldog clip (as shown in the illustration). Alternatively, the games can be stored in boxes – either kept individually or grouped according to difficulty in a large box and separated using coloured dividers.

ADAPTING THE GAMES

Photocopiable games are easily adapted. They can be changed to suit different purposes and abilities. You need not be stuck with a resource that only meets a small percentage of your requirements. Just delete the bit you don't want by covering with liquid paper or a sticky label, then draw and/or print your modification on top. If you are altering very fine detail, enlarge the sheet before making the alterations. Do your alterations on the enlargement, making sure to draw the lines the same density and thickness as the enlargement. Then reduce back to original size. Similarly, if a game is too big or too small, it can be altered to size using the enlarging or reducing facility on large photocopiers. If yours won't do this, ones that will can be found in most public libraries.

Simple alterations such as writing children's names on playing pieces or using the school logo on the headings may seem small things in themselves, but they make the games more personal and special.

Copies of each adaptation can be kept in polypockets in an A4 ring binder devoted to the purpose. A slip of paper or card can be put in the pocket detailing when the adaptation was made, its curriculum focus, which class used it, notes on how effective it was and further ideas for adaptation.

CROSS-CURRICULAR CONNECTIONS

As many of the games involve role-playing and have suitable contexts to develop storylines, they fit easily into language topics. Some of the games will readily integrate with other subject areas – for example, 'Square meal' with science and 'Supermarket' with geography.

LINKS TO THE NATIONAL CURRICULUM

● main game
○ extension

Games	Programme of Study																	
	1a	1b	1c	2a	2b	2c	3a	3b	3c	3d	3e	3f	3g	3h	4a	4b	4c	HD2	HD3
Next in line				●	○				○										
Make £1					○				●	●					●				
Good guess!	●								●	●				●					
Odds and evens							●		●	●									
Criss cross									●										
Make a multiple									●										
Fizz! Buzz!					●				●	●									
Four square																●	●		
Name your number										●					●		●		
What number am I?	●						●		●										
Eye spy a big number		●		●															
At the cinema									●										
Bags of numbers			●				●		●	●					●				
Supermarket					●										●				
Make a fiver		●			●					●						●			
Coin hopscotch		●			●						●		●	●	●		●		
Box office		●			●	○				●								○	
City traffic																		●	
Square meal					●				●						●	●			
What's the difference?			●				●					●		●	●		●		
Noughty		●		●			●			●					●		●		
Skyline				●	●					○			○						
100 squares/sequences							●		●										
100 triangle diamonds							●		●										
Carpet tiles								●											
Palace in Numberland									●										
Mt. Probability																		●	●
Grand Prix							●		●										
Super saver day				●											●				
Number roulette		●			●					○			●	○	○		●	●	
Choc shop					●	●									●		●		
Number monorail					●			●											
Remainders										●	●								
Summit									●	●			●		●		●		
Acrobats	●	●					●		●					●					

Number
INTRODUCTION

LINKS TO SCOTTISH 5–14 GUIDELINES

● main game
○ extension

Attainment target and outcomes

Games	RTN B	RTN C	RTN D/E	PS B	PS C	AS B	AS C	AS D	MB	MC	MD B	MD C	MD D	FE B	FE C	FE D	FPR	SPM	IH
Next in line	●	○					○			○									
Make £1						●	○		●	○									
Good guess!						●													
Odds and evens				●		●	●												
Criss cross												●							
Make a multiple						●						●							
Fizz! Buzz!	●				●							●							
Four square						●						●			●				
Name your number						●	●					●	●						
What number am I?					●	●						●			●	●			
Eye spy a big number	●																		
At the cinema						●													
Bags of numbers	●			●		●		●											
Supermarket		●					●					○							
Make a fiver	●	●				●				●									
Coin hopscotch						●	●		●	●									●
Box office		●				●						●							○
City traffic																			●
Square meal		●	●			●				●									
What's the difference?		●				●								●					
Noughty	●					●						●	●	●					●
Skyline		●						○								●			
100 squares/sequences				●										●	●				
100 triangle diamonds				●										●	●				
Carpet tiles																	●		
Palace in Numberland												●							
Mt. Probability																			●
Grand Prix																			●
Super saver day		●	●																
Number roulette		●						○											●
Choc shop		●														●			
Number monorail		●																	
Remainders								●				●							
Summit					●	●	●	●			●	●	●						
Acrobats			●									●			●				

12

MATHS GAMES
KEY STAGE TWO

Activity games

NEXT IN LINE

WHAT YOU NEED
Card, a black felt-tipped pen, paper and pencils (for extensions only).

TEACHING CONTENT
☆ Reading and ordering whole numbers (N: 2a; RTN: B)

PREPARATION
Decide on the range of numbers you want the children to practise. Prepare number cards (enough for each child in the class to have one) by writing a different number on each card within a chosen range.

HOW TO PLAY
Divide the class into two teams and put a stack of cards, number side down, in front of each team. Each team member takes a card and hides it behind his or her back. When the teacher says 'Go', the children reveal their numbers and, in their teams, have to sort themselves into a number line from lowest to highest. The first team to do this correctly scores a point. The first team to score five points (or any other set limit) wins.

TEACHER'S ROLE
The game can be applied to any range of numbers, and these do not necessarily have to be in consecutive order.

After the game, ask the teams to sit down with their number cards. Each team has gaps in its line. Ask the children to identify the missing numbers. What gaps are there in Team A? What numbers would fill the gaps? Who would need to leave Team B in order to fill the gaps in Team A? Do the same for Team B. Organise the children into a class line and tell them to sit down. Ask various number sequences to stand up – for example, all the even numbers; all the odd numbers; all the numbers divisible by 2, 5 or 10.

EXTENSIONS
☆ Developing understanding of place value (N: 2a; RTN: B)
☆ Working with decimals to two decimal places in the context of money (N: 2b; RTN: C; M: C)

Make cards with money notation on them. Do the children understand that £1.05 is less than £1.50?

☆ Practising addition and subtraction facts within a given range of numbers (N: 3c; AS: C)

For this game, the children have to work in pairs within their team to perform either an addition or a subtraction operation with their numbers *before* ordering the results. Choose an appropriate range of numbers for the cards, and tell the children whether you want them to add or subtract. Make sure there is an even number of children on each team. After the team members have chosen their cards but before they reveal them, they should each pair up with someone else on their team and each pair should be given a piece of paper and pencil. They then reveal their numbers and the partners either add or subtract them as the teacher indicates. The pairs make a new card with the resulting number, and then order themselves from lowest to highest.

The game proceeds as above.

Number ACTIVITY GAMES

WHAT YOU NEED
A large collection of coins (all denominations from 1p to 50p), a till (optional), a coin dice and shaker.

MAKE £1

TEACHING CONTENT
☆ Practising addition with whole numbers up to 100 (N: 3c, d; AS: B)
☆ Using coins up to £1 (N: 4a; M: B)

PREPARATION
Ensure that the children have had experience of handling all six coins, know their values and understand that £1 equals 100 pence. Make a large coin dice out of a play brick with different card coins stuck on each face, as shown below. For fun, use a large plant pot as a shaker.

HOW TO PLAY
This is a game for the whole class, divided into small groups of 4 or 5 children. The aim is to be the first group to make £1 from the six types of coin. Any combination is permitted as long as it makes exactly £1, no more or less.

Sit the groups around a central 'bank' of money (a toy till is ideal). The dice and shaker are passed from group to group. The groups take turns throwing the coin dice and taking the coin shown. Children within a group should take turns throwing the dice when it is their group's turn, so that everyone gets a chance to participate. If a group does not want the coin thrown, it does not have to take it; but once taken it must be kept. If a coin is rejected, that throw is wasted and the dice goes on to the next group. Coins are accumulated until a group calls out 'Pound!' The coins are laid out in order of value and the teacher checks them, making a note of how the £1 was made. The winning group sits still while the game is resumed until another £1 is made. *This must be different from the one already made.* The game goes on until all groups have made £1.

TEACHER'S ROLE
Make sure that all the children in each group are having a go and that no one child is dominating. Listen and observe in order to assess the mental methods being used. As each group makes its £1, write a corresponding number sentence on the board. For example:

1p		2p		5p		10p		20p		50p	=	£1
1p	+	4p	+	5p	+	20p	+	20p	+	50p	=	100p

15

At the end of the game, discuss with the children the different ways the groups found of making £1. Make a class chart showing the various ways. Can they think of any other ways?

EXTENSION

★ Extending mental methods of addition with numbers beyond 100 (N: 3d; AS: C)
★ Using coins and notes beyond £1 (N: 2b, 4a; M: C)

Make the aim of the game to accumulate as much money as possible in a set number of throws, say 10. After each group has had their ten throws, they work out how much they have accumulated. The group with the most money wins.

GOOD GUESS!

TEACHING CONTENT

★ Developing flexible and effective methods of computation (N: 1a)
★ Subtracting mentally with numbers to 6 (N: 3c; AS: B)
★ Adding mentally with totals to 50 (N: 3c, d; AS: B)
★ Using a calculator (N: 3h; RTN: A)

PREPARATION

If you are playing this with the whole class, make four sets of cards numbered 1 to 6, each large enough to be seen by the whole group. For smaller groups, you could use the 1 to 6 cards only from a deck of cards.

Give each child a piece of paper and pencil. Ask them to make a 3-column grid with the headings Guess, Card and Difference, as shown in the illustration below. Tell them to divide the grid into 10 rows.

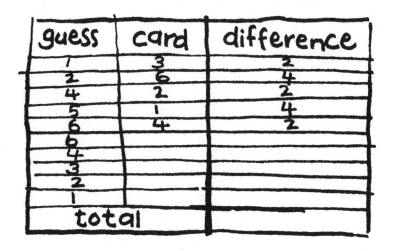

HOW TO PLAY

Shuffle the cards and place them face down in front of you. Tell the children that the pile of cards contains four each of the numbers 1 to 6. Ask them to guess what the first ten cards will be, and to write their guesses in order in the left-hand column of their grid. Now turn over the top card. If this card is a 3, for instance, the children should write 3 in the top row of the middle column on their grid. They then work out the

WHAT YOU NEED
FOR CONSTRUCTION
Paper and pencils (enough for the whole class), card, scissors, a black felt-tipped pen.
FOR PLAYING
A prepared grid and pencil per player, four sets of cards numbered 1 to 6 (for a small group, these could be from a deck of playing cards), a calculator (optional).

difference between their guess and the actual card, and put this result in the Difference column. Now turn over the next card and repeat the procedure, until ten cards have been turned over. The children then total the numbers in their Difference column. The winner is the player who has the lowest total and is therefore the best guesser.

TEACHER'S ROLE

You may need to remind the children that they cannot list a number more than four times in their Guess column, since there are only four of each number in the pack. Although the children will be most concerned with the accuracy of their guesses, you will want to assess the accuracy of their computation. Do they understand that to find the difference, they have to subtract? Do they realise that they have to subtract the smaller number from the larger number, no matter which column it is in? Which children are not yet able to calculate mentally? You may need to help some children with totalling the Difference column at the end, as this involves adding ten numbers together. Use it as an opportunity to discuss different methods. Have a calculator on hand to show how you can use it to check totals. You could ask the children to swap grids with each other in order to check their calculations.

ODDS AND EVENS

TEACHING CONTENT

★ Reinforcing odd and even numbers and developing understanding of how they combine to give odd or even numbers (N: 3a; PS: B)
★ Practising addition (N: 3c, d; AS: B, C)

PREPARATION

The children should be capable of mentally adding three single-digit numbers.

WHAT YOU NEED
A chalkboard, chalk.

HOW TO PLAY

Divide the class into two teams. One team is the Odds team and can use the numbers 1, 3, 5, 7 and 9. The other team is the Evens team and can use the numbers 2, 4, 6 and 8. Draw a noughts and crosses grid on the board and set the children a target number, say 15. Begin with the Odds team. Choose one member of the team and ask which of their odd numbers they'd like to play and where on the grid they want to place it. Then do the same with the Evens team. The teams take it in turns to play and can only use each number once. The first team to make the total of 15 in any row (horizontally, vertically or diagonally) wins. Play again, using a different total and swapping the odds and evens teams.

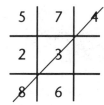 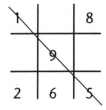

TEACHER'S ROLE

During the game, question the children about their strategy in choosing and placing their numbers on the grid. Is the target number odd or even? How can they tell? (*By looking at the units digit.*) If the target number is an even number, which combinations of odd and even numbers can they have? (*3 evens; 2 odds and 1 even.*) What about if the target number is an odd number? (*3 odds; 2 evens and 1 odd.*)

CRISS CROSS

TEACHING CONTENT

☆ Practising multiplication facts to 10 x 10 (N: 3c; MD: C)
☆ Developing an understanding of the reciprocal nature of multiplication facts (N: 3c; MD: C)

PREPARATION

Two versions of this game are given. For the first version, two number bags each containing a set of 1 to 10 number cards are needed. These can be made up from photocopiable sheet 34. Copy the sheet directly on to card, or mount on to card after copying. Then cut up to make individual number cards. For the second version a set of 37 (or 42 if you want to include the 1× table) A4-sized product cards is needed. These represent all the possible products from the 2× (or 1×) to 10× tables. You will also need to draw a large chalk multiplication sign on the floor for the children to sit along, as in the illustration below.

WHAT YOU NEED

PHOTOCOPIABLE SHEETS
Number cards (1) 34 (first version).

FOR CONSTRUCTION
Card, scissors, glue, a black felt-tipped pen (second version).

FOR PLAYING
A large space, chalk, paper, pencils, two bags of 1 to 10 number cards (first version), 37 or 42 (if including 1× table) product cards (second version).

Before starting the game, ask the children to work in pairs to make up a table triangle similar to the completed one below. When they have drawn the table, ask them to circle any repeated numbers (leaving only one appearance for each number). How many numbers are left? (*37, or 42 if 1× table is included.*) These are the basic products for the 2× (1×) to 10× tables. Discuss the reciprocal nature of multiplication facts: for example, that 3 × 4 has the same product as 4 × 3.

X	10	9	8	7	6	5	4	3	2
2	20	18	16	14	12	10	8	6	4
3	30	27	24	21	(18)	15	(12)	9	
4	40	36	32	28	(24)	(20)	(16)		
5	50	45	(40)	35	(30)	25			
6	60	54	48	42	(36)				
7	70	63	56	49					
8	80	72	64						
9	90	81							
10	100								

HOW TO PLAY

First version: Divide the class into two teams. Two children, or the teacher and one child, are chosen to draw the digits from the bags. The teams sit on opposite sides of the multiplication sign, with team members sitting one behind the other. The two digit-drawers sit on the other two sides of the sign. In turn, each takes out a card from her bag and holds it up. The first player on each team must try to be the first to say what the product of the two numbers is. The first correct answer scores a point for that team. The teacher keeps score. The digit cards are replaced in the bags, and the first players then move to the back of their lines. It is now the turn of the second team member in each team. Play continues until all team members have had a go. The points are then totalled and the team with the most points wins.

Second version: Divide the class into four teams and tell them to sit in lines along the arms of the cross as shown in the illustration. If one or more teams are shorter than the others, one player can take a double turn. The product number cards are shuffled and placed in a stack face down in the centre of the cross. The teacher turns over the top card, and the first player from each team competes with the other first players to give the two numbers (multiplier and multiplicand) which make this product. Players must raise their hands rather than shout out the answer. The first player to give the correct answer scores a point for her team. If the product can be made in more than one way (e.g. 18 = 9 × 2 and 6 × 3), a bonus point may be given if the player can also give the alternative.

TEACHER'S ROLE

In the first version, make a note of which (if any) number combinations are causing trouble and revise these with the children. In the second version, encourage children to look at number patterns and discover 'short cuts'. For example, if an even number up to 20 is shown, 2 is a certain multiplier with 2, 4, 6, 8 and 10 as possible second numbers.

Similarly '3s' numbers can be identified by adding all the digits and dividing by 3, while in '9s' numbers (up to 90) the digits add up to 9. And of course, '5s' end in 5 or 0 and '10s' in 0. If appropriate, introduce the children to the relevant vocabulary: product, multiplier, multiplicand.

GAME VARIATION

The second version of the game can also be played using division. The same cards are used, and the players have to state two numbers that will divide evenly into the number drawn.

MAKE A MULTIPLE

TEACHING CONTENT
★ Practising continuous addition with single-digit numbers (N: 3c; AS: C)
★ Developing knowledge of multiplication tables to 10 (N: 3c; MD: C)

PREPARATION
If you are playing this game with a large group or whole class, you will need to make four sets of 1 to 6 number cards, each big enough for the whole class to see. For smaller groups, the 24 cards from a deck of playing cards will do.

HOW TO PLAY

This is a game for two teams. The aim of the game is to create multiples of a given number by adding card numbers together.

Divide the class into two teams, A and B. Tell them which multiplication table they are playing with. Let's say you have chosen to practise the 4× table. Shuffle the 24 cards, then take ten cards from the top and place them blank side forward along the chalkboard ledge. The first player from Team A comes up and turns over one card at a time. The number on the second card is added to the number on the first, that total is added to the third card, and so on. If a total is reached that is a multiple of 4, the team scores a point. Continue until all ten cards have been turned over. Now it is the turn of the first player on Team B. Reshuffle the cards and continue as before. When all the players on both teams have had a go, the team with the most points is the winner.

1st card	2nd card	3rd card	4th card	5th card	etc.
5 +	4 +	3 +	2 +	2	
		[=12: score]		[=16: score]	etc.

TEACHER'S ROLE
Play this game when a particular multiplication table needs practice or general revision. As each player on a team has an individual go, it is an excellent opportunity to assess children's mental addition and ability to recognise multiples of the designated number. However, as this is a team

WHAT YOU NEED
FOR CONSTRUCTION
Card, scissors, a black felt-tipped pen.
FOR PLAYING
Four sets of cards numbered 1 to 6 (for a small group, these could be from a deck of playing cards).

game, help can be given by team members, which should support (rather than isolate) the child with less confidence. During play, ask questions such as: What is the total now? What number would you need to turn over next to get a multiple of 4?

FIZZ! BUZZ!

WHAT YOU NEED
A large space, copies of hundred square, coloured pencils (optional).

TEACHING CONTENT

☆ Ordering whole numbers to 100 (N: 2a; RTN: B)
☆ Recognising number patterns (N: 3a; PS: C)
☆ Practising multiplication facts to 10 × 10 (N:3c; MD: C)

HOW TO PLAY

This game, which practises multiples of specific numbers, is ideal for the whole class. Ask the children to sit in a circle. Choose two multiplication tables to practise, for example 3 and 4. The children take it in turns to count numbers out loud, beginning with 1. For example, the first child says '1', the next child says '2', the next '3', and so on. When the counting reaches a multiple of 3, the child for that number must call out 'Fizz!' instead of the number. When they come to a number in the 4 times table, they have to call out 'Buzz!' instead of the number. When they come to a number that is in both the 3 times and the 4 times tables (for example, 12), they have to say 'Fizz! Buzz!' How far can they get without making a mistake? If you want to have a single winner, state that those players who get it wrong are out and the winner is the last one left.

TEACHER'S ROLE

Although this game can be played with the whole class, you may prefer the children to work in ability groups. After playing, give pairs of children a copy of a hundred square (see photocopiable page 83) and ask them to colour in the numbers in the three times and four times tables. They should use one colour for the three times table, another for the four times table and a third colour for those numbers which appear in both. Is there a regular pattern? If so, can they explain it?

GAME VARIATION

With children who are less confident with tables, let them work in smaller groups and with only one times table at a time. Instead of saying 'Fizz!' or 'Buzz!', let them make up their own word, such as 'Zap!'

FOUR SQUARE

TEACHING CONTENT

★ Choosing sequences of suitable computational methods appropriate to a problem, adapting them and applying them accurately (N: 4b; AS: C; MD: C)
★ Checking results by different methods and estimating and approximating solutions to problems (N: 4c)
★ Using a simple 'function machine' for operations involving doubling, halving, adding and subtracting (FE: C)

PREPARATION

A large indoor space such as a school hall is needed. Make a set of large 1 to 10 number cards, enough for one per child. Divide the children into teams of 4, and for each team chalk a large square on the floor. Place a number card face down in each corner of each square.

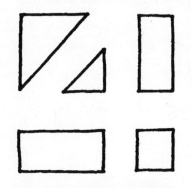

WHAT YOU NEED

FOR CONSTRUCTION
Scissors, card, a black felt-tipped pen.

FOR PLAYING
A large playing space, chalk, a set of 1 to 10 number cards (enough for one per player).

HOW TO PLAY

Tell each team to choose a square, and each team member to stand by one of the four cards in the corners. At a given signal from the teacher, each child turns over his card. Each team now has to arrange the numbers to get as big a number as possible, following these simple rules: two corners have to be added together, while the other two corners have to be subtracted. The two resulting numbers are then multiplied together to give the final total. The children need to remember the total as well as how they calculated it.

TEACHER'S ROLE

When all the teams have completed their calculations, check each in turn, discussing with the class the various computational methods. Could the number arrangement be improved to get a bigger final number? Get children to experiment with ordered combinations of the four numbers. For example, addition with numbers 7, 9, 3 and 1:

7 + 9 = 16   9 + 7 = 16   3 + 9 = 12   1 + 9 = 10
7 + 3 = 10   9 + 3 = 12   3 + 7 = 10   1 + 7 = 8
7 + 1 = 8   9 + 1 = 10   3 + 1 = 4   1 + 3 = 4

And then subtraction, and so on. This could be set as a class puzzle.

GAME VARIATIONS

Play the game as above, but ask the teams to try to get as low a number as possible.

NAME YOUR NUMBER

TEACHING CONTENT
★ Developing the use of the four operations to solve problems (N: 4a; AS: C, D; MD: C, D)
★ Developing a sense of the size of a solution (N: 4c)
★ Developing a variety of mental methods of computation (N: 3d)

PREPARATION

Give each child a sticky label and a pen or pencil. Explain to them that they are going to give themselves new names, and that these names will be numbers. For example, your old name was Kate Jones, but your new name is 45. Nellie Lim's new name is 63. Christopher Newman's new name is 116. Can the children figure out how to work out their new names? (*The tens place numeral is the number of letters in their first name, and the units place numeral is the number of letters in their surname. If either part of the name is more than 9 letters long, an additional digit is added to the new name. For example, the name Alison Dziemianowicz becomes 613 and* ***not*** *73.*)

Go round the group and ask each child in turn what his or her new name is. Tell them to write their new names on their labels, and to stick these on their chests so everyone can see them. Are there any children with the same new name? If so, are they all boys or girls, or not? Ask the children to line up in numerical order. Then choose alternate children to form Team A and Team B.

HOW TO PLAY

Tell the teams to stand opposite each other in two semicircles, so that they can all see each other's new name labels. Explain that you will give them a name problem to solve. The first person to raise their hand and give the correct answer will earn a point for their team. The problems should involve names of children in the group, and should reflect their mathematical ability. For example:
- What is Nellie Lim (*63*) subtracted from Christopher Newman (*116*)? (*53.*)
- What is Sanjay Gupta (*65*) added to Matthew Brownlow (*78*)? (*143.*)
- What is one-half of Matthew Brownlow? (*39.*)

If the team that wins the point also has a member whose number name is the same as the answer, that team gets a bonus point. The first team to reach 10 points (or any other predetermined limit) is the winner.

TEACHER'S ROLE

You will need to assess the children's level of ability in order to determine which mathematical operations you can use. The children will need to listen very carefully, so make sure it is completely quiet when you state each problem. When a child has given a correct answer, ask her to explain how she worked it out. Children will have developed different mental methods, and it is useful to share these.

WHAT YOU NEED
Sticky labels and pens or pencils (enough for one per player).

Number
ACTIVITY GAMES

WHAT NUMBER AM I?

WHAT YOU NEED
No special equipment required.

TEACHING CONTENT

★ Developing flexible and effect methods of computation and using them with understanding (N: 1a)
★ Using words to describe and explain number relationships (N: 3a; PS: C; FE: C, D)
★ Using the four operations and a variety of mental methods of computation (N: 3d; AS: C; MD: C)

HOW TO PLAY

This is a game for two teams, who compete to gain points by answering number questions devised by their opponents.

Divide the group into two teams, A and B. Ask the first player from Team A to think of a number. She should not say it out loud, but whisper it to you. She should then think of a question to ask Team B, the answer to which is her number. For example, if her chosen number is 34, she could ask: What number am I if I am 6 less than 40? Or she could ask: What number am I if I am 5 times 6 plus 4? If someone on Team B gives the correct answer, Team B scores a point. If not, Team A scores that point. Next, a player from Team B thinks of a number and asks Team A a question. And so on, until all the players have had a go. The team with the most points at the end wins.

TEACHER'S ROLE

The advantage of this game is that the level of play is determined by each individual player. The questions can be as simple or as difficult as the questioner is capable of mathematically. It is important that their chosen number is whispered to you, so that you can check that the question fits the answer. Depending on the ability of the group as a whole, you may wish to provide model questions when introducing the game. For example, you may want to limit the range of numbers chosen and/or the operations involved in the questions. You may, for instance, wish the range to be from 1 to 20 and questions to involve only addition and subtraction. Give the children a model question. For example, you could say: 'I have chosen the number 18, so I could ask: What number am I if I am 3 more than 15? Or I could ask: What number am I if I am 20 take away 2?'

Photocopiable games

MATHS GAMES
KEY STAGE TWO

EYE SPY A BIG NUMBER

TEACHING CONTENT

★ Reading, writing and ordering whole numbers up to 100, understanding that the position of a digit signifies its value (N: 2a; RTN: B)
★ Using practical resources as tools for exploring number structure (N:1b)

PREPARATION

You will need to construct the Eye spy meter from the Special section (pages 138 and 139). Ideally, there should be a meter for each player.

HOW TO PLAY

This is a game for two or more players, and the aim is to get the highest number. Ideally, each player should have an Eye spy meter of his own, but the game can be played with one that is passed from player to player. The eyes on the meter are set to 00. Players take it in turns to throw the dice up to three times for each eye, starting with the right eye. The players do not have to use all three throws for each eye. If, for example, a player throws a 3 on her first dice throw and a 6 on her second, she will have a maximum score of 9 and will want to stop there. When a player has thrown for both eyes, she fills in her record sheet and the next player has his turn. After everyone has had a go, the player with the highest number wins.

TEACHER'S ROLE

Although this game is relatively simple, the children do have decisions to make about when to stop the number wheels. They have three chances per wheel, so they have to be aware of the ascending value of each digit. For example, a pupil who got a 9 in the 'right eye' (i.e. the units window) on the second go and opted to throw for a third time would display a lack of knowledge of basic number values and/or the limitations of throwing a 1 to 6 dice, as the highest digit he could then get in the 'right eye' would be 5 (if he threw a 6 on his third throw).

During the game, note which children have difficulty with the values of single digits and/or with the concept of counting on after the dice throw. Ask questions to assess their knowledge of the values of the numbers they have on their meter. Can they combine the 'right eye' and 'left eye' numbers to read the resulting number? Can they say why this number is higher or lower than another player's?

WHAT YOU NEED

PHOTOCOPIABLE SHEETS
Eye spy clown face sheet 138, Eye spy number wheels sheet 139, 'How to play' sheet 27, record sheet 28.

FOR CONSTRUCTION
Card, glue, scissors, 2 paper fasteners or card rivets.

FOR PLAYING
Eye spy meter (preferably one for each player), 'How to play' sheet, record sheet and pencil, dice and shaker.

HOW TO PLAY EYE SPY A BIG NUMBER

For 2 or more players.

YOU NEED: Eye spy meter (preferably one for each player), record sheet and pencil, dice and shaker.

❶ Each player should have an Eye spy meter and a game record strip. (If only one meter is available, it can be passed from player to player.) The aim of the game is to make the highest number.

❷ The first player sets the eyes on his meter to 00. He then throws the dice and moves the right eye wheel to that number. The player may stop on that number, but if he wants to try for a higher number he can throw the dice again and move the wheel on. A player can throw a maximum of three times for each eye.

For example, a player throws a 3 on his first go. He moves the right eye wheel to 3 and decides to throw again. His second throw is a 1. He moves the right eye wheel on 1, so it now reads 4. He decides to throw for a third time and throws another 4. The right eye now reads 8. If, however, he had thrown a 6 on his third throw, the right eye would now read 0!

❸ The player does the same for the left eye.

❹ When the player has made the highest two-digit number he can, he writes this on his game record strip.

❺ The other players take it in turn to do the same.

❻ When everyone has had a go, the player with the highest number wins.

☆ REMEMBER!

Players can throw the dice up to 3 times for each eye, but do not have to use all three throws if they do not want to.

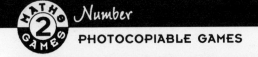

Number
PHOTOCOPIABLE GAMES

■ SCHOLASTIC PHOTOCOPIABLES

EYE SPY A BIG NUMBER

RECORD SHEET FOR EYE SPY A BIG NUMBER

Name

My meter made this number.

Name

My meter made this number.

Name

My meter made this number.

AT THE CINEMA

TEACHING CONTENT

★ Consolidating addition and subtraction facts to 20 (N: 3c; AS: B)

PREPARATION

Photocopy sheets 31 and 32 on to card. A piece of card 40cm × 25cm[?] is also needed as the base for the cinema. See the diagram below for construction of the cinema. Cut up sheet 32 to make individual spectator playing pieces; colour and fold as indicated. A four-colour dice is needed to match the playing pieces. Stick labels on to the sides of a building block or standard dice and colour these in with pens or pencils. The remaining two faces should be left 'white' to add an extra dimension to the game (it may be best if these are opposite faces).

HOW TO PLAY

This is a game for four players. Each player chooses one of the coloured sets (red, blue, green or yellow) and collects all of the spectator playing pieces in that colour. The players take turns to throw the colour dice. If a player throws his own colour, or white, he can place one of his own spectators on a seat in the cinema. If he throws one of the other colours, then only the player with that colour set can place a spectator on a seat in the cinema. Play continues until all of the available seats in the cinema are filled. The player who has the largest number of spectators in their colour in the cinema is the winner.

TEACHER'S ROLE

Make sure the children understand which player is entitled to place one of the spectators in each turn. Where have they placed the spectator? Which row? Which number seat? Ask players to keep track of how many spectators they each have in the cinema. Who is winning? How many spectators are there in the cinema altogether? How many empty spaces are there? Highlight the progression of these two totals as the game is being played to help the children understand the inverse relationship between addition and subtraction. A copy of photocopiable sheet 31 can be used as a record sheet on which each child colours in the seats he has bought. Players can then count up the number of seats in their colour in each row and fill in the number sentence for each row. These number sentences can then be used to investigate number bonds to 10. Ask questions to develop this. How many red seats are there in row A? How many in the whole cinema? If all of the 'red' spectators left the cinema, how many empty seats would there be in each row? This strategy can be extended to investigate number bonds to 20 and to 30. If you wish, you can incorporate a screen element in the cinema construction and the children can illustrate filmstrips to be shown to the cinema audience.

GAME VARIATION

The 'reserved' cards can be used to change the total of seats available and thus vary the numbers involved in the game. They can be placed before starting the game; or alternatively, the white faces of the dice can be labelled 'R', and when these are rolled a 'reserved' card is used.

WHAT YOU NEED

PHOTOCOPIABLE SHEETS
Cinema seats sheet 31, 'How to play' sheet 30, spectator playing pieces sheet 32.

FOR CONSTRUCTION
Card, scissors, glue, adhesive tape, sticky labels, coloured pens or pencils, a dice or building block.

FOR PLAYING
A cinema game board, a set of playing pieces in a different colour for each player (red, blue, green and yellow), 'How to play' sheet, a colour dice and shaker.

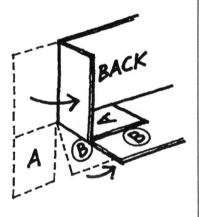

Assemble the rows of the seats as shown above then stick to the baseboard. A cinema screen can be included for added effect.

HOW TO PLAY AT THE CINEMA

For 4 players.

YOU NEED: a cinema game board, a complete set of spectator playing pieces, a colour dice and shaker.

❶ Each player chooses a colour (red, blue, green or yellow) and collects that set of spectator playing pieces.

❷ Take turns to throw the colour dice. If you throw your own colour, or white, you can place one of your spectators on a seat in the cinema. If you throw another colour, only the player with that colour can place one of his spectators in the cinema.

So: if you are blue and you throw green, only the player with the green set of spectators can place a spectator in the cinema.

❸ Continue playing until all of the seats in the cinema are taken.

❹ Count up how many spectators there are of each colour in the cinema. The player with the highest total is the winner.

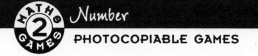

CINEMA SEATS

Cut out each row of seats. See page 29 for construction instructions.

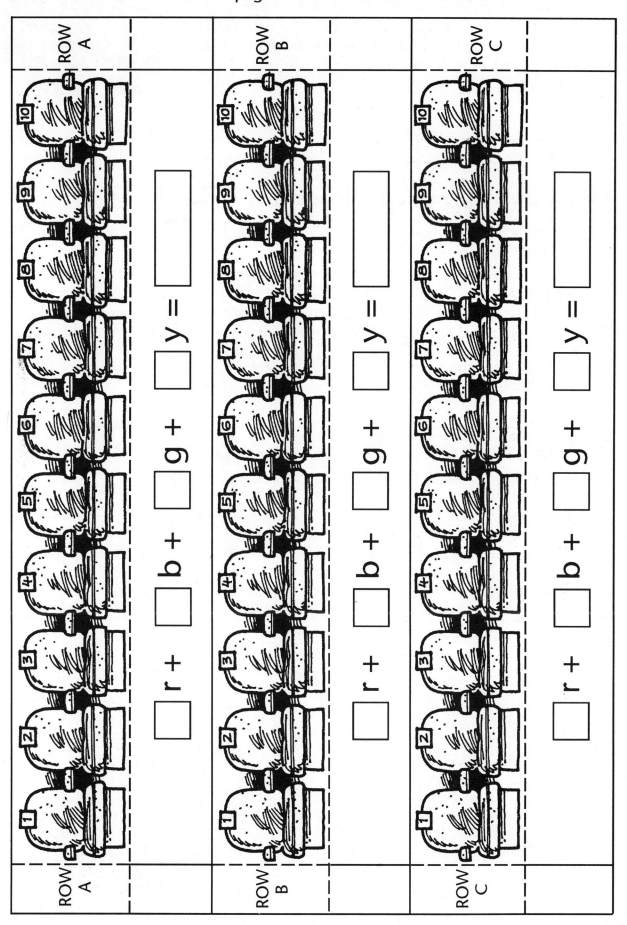

SPECTATOR PLAYING PIECES

Colour all of the spectators on this sheet in the same colour (red, blue, green or yellow) so that there is one complete set in each colour. Cut up this sheet to make individual cards and fold along the dotted lines as shown.

x4

BAGS OF NUMBERS

WHAT YOU NEED
PHOTOCOPIABLE SHEETS
Number cards sheets 34 and 35, coin cards sheet 36.
FOR CONSTRUCTION
Card, glue, scissors.
FOR PLAYING
Single digit and double digit number cards, coin cards, three bags.

TEACHING CONTENT
★ Reading and ordering whole numbers up to 100 and then to 1000 (N: 2a; RTN: B)
★ Exploring number patterns and sequences (N: 3a; PS: B)
★ Practising and developing a variety of methods for adding and subtracting (N: 3c, d; AS: B)
★ Using coins up to £1 (N: 4a; M: B)

PREPARATION
Photocopy pages 34 and 35 (number cards) and page 36 (coin cards) directly on to card, or mount them on to card after copying. Then cut them up to make individual cards. The numbers from 1 to 9 inclusive can be kept in one bag (the single digits bag), and the numbers from 10 to 99 can be kept in another (the double digits bag). The coins can be kept in yet another bag.

HOW TO PLAY
The purpose of number (or coin) cards is to allow random selection of numbers, when the range to be used is greater than can be catered for by dice or a spinner. By using both single digit and double digit bags together, numbers over 99 and up to 999 can be made. The coin cards avoid the problem, inherent in using real coins, of recognition by touch. It is too easy to *feel* the difference in the various coins when picking randomly from a bag. The following are some game ideas using the bags of numbers and coins:

Biggest/smallest hundred number: Use both the single digit and double digit bags. In turn, draw one single digit number and one double digit number and make as big/small a hundred number as possible. The single digit number can be used in front of or behind the double digit number.

Number pattern or sequence: Use one or both bags. In turn, draw numbers and keep them until someone can make a pattern or sequence using three cards. Later extend to four cards. Arbitrate if the pattern is not clear.

Add on/take away: Use both the single digit and double digit bags. In turn, draw one single digit number and one double digit number and add the two together. The player who makes the biggest number wins. A more difficult version is to use two double digit numbers. Alternatively, players could subtract the single digit from the double digit number, or find the difference between two double digit numbers.

Four ways: Use both the single digit and double digit bags. In turn, draw one single digit number and one double digit number, and make four number sentences (including answers) using the four operations.

Collect a set: Use the bag of coin cards. In turn, draw cards from the bag. If you already have the coin shown, put it back. Otherwise keep it. The first player to get a full set of coins (1p, 2p, 5p, 10p, 20p, 50p, £1) wins.

Loads of money: Use the bag of coin cards. In a predetermined set number of draws, who can get the most money?

NUMBER CARDS (1)
Cut up this sheet to make individual number cards.

1	2	3	4	5	6	7	8
9	1	2	3	4	5	6	7
8	9	1	2	3	4	5	6
7	8	9	1	2	3	4	5
6	7	8	9	1	2	3	4
5	6	7	8	9	1	2	3
4	5	6	7	8	9	10	11
12	13	14	15	16	17	18	19
20	21	22	23	24	25	26	27

NUMBER CARDS (2)
Cut up this sheet to make individual number cards.

28	29	30	31	32	33	34	35
36	37	38	39	40	41	42	43
44	45	46	47	48	49	50	51
52	53	54	55	56	57	58	59
60	61	62	63	64	65	66	67
68	69	70	71	72	73	74	75
76	77	78	79	80	81	82	83
84	85	86	87	88	89	90	91
92	93	94	95	96	97	98	99

COIN CARDS

SUPERMARKET

TEACHING CONTENT

★ Adding numbers to two decimal places in the context of money (N: 2b; AS: D)
★ Using the functions of a basic calculator to work out mathematical problems (N: 4a; RTN: C)

PREPARATION

Assembling the game: Photocopy pages 40, 41 and 42 on to card and assemble the supermarket game board as indicated below. The shelves of the supermarket can be coloured in before assembly to make the game board more attractive. If you wish, a 'wall' can be included as an extension of the baseboard so that the supermarket has entrance and exit doors. Colour in the shopping trolley playing pieces, then cut them out, fold them and stick them together as indicated on page 39. The record sheet on page 43 can be photocopied on to paper, as it can only be used once.

Introducing the game: Most children will have visited a supermarket and be familiar with how they are laid out and how shoppers walk up and down the aisles in order to purchase the items that they require. Have the children been shopping with their family? Did they use a shopping list? Did they look at the price of each item as they took it from the shelves? Did they use a calculator to work out how much money was being spent, or wait to see the total at the checkout? It may be useful to discuss the board with the children before playing the game, to make sure that they can identify each item and understand how to read and write the prices given.

HOW TO PLAY

This is a game for two to four players. Each player needs a copy of record sheet 43, one of the coloured shopping trolley playing pieces and a pencil. The players take turns to roll the dice and, starting from the entrance to the supermarket, move their shopping trolley along the track according to the number thrown. They must then buy the item on the square on which they have landed, and record this by filling in the price of each item they buy on their record sheet. Play continues until all of the players have completed the journey along the supermarket track; then they all add up the total value of the items that they have bought. The player with the highest total is the winner.

TEACHER'S ROLE

This game is fairly straightforward, and it is only at the end that any complex calculation is required. As the game is being played, ask the children questions to develop their counting skills and recognition and recording of money values. How many items have you bought so far? How many items did you buy in the first/second/third aisle? How much is the jam (or any other item they have just bought) worth? How do you write this amount? Which digits go to the left of the decimal point on the record sheet? Watch carefully to make sure the children understand how to record the decimal amounts correctly. It is important that all of the

WHAT YOU NEED

PHOTOCOPIABLE PAGES
Supermarket baseboard sheet 40, supermarket aisle sheets 41 and 42, shopping trolley playing pieces and 'How to play' sheet 39, record sheet 43.

FOR CONSTRUCTION
Card, scissors, adhesive, coloured crayons.

FOR PLAYING
Supermarket game board, 'How to play' sheet, a shopping trolley playing piece for each player, a record sheet and pencil for each player, a dice and shaker, a calculator.

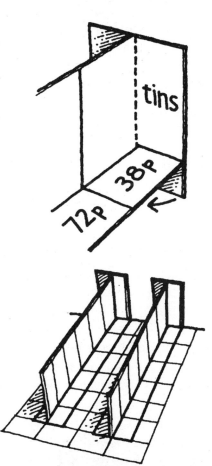

Assemble the four aisles as shown above. Stick two copies of the baseboard (page 40) side-by-side and fix the aisles in place.

prices should be recorded as decimal figures. Point the children in the right direction if they encounter difficulties – it may be best if they record their entries in pencil, so that any mistakes can easily be corrected. If recording the amounts interferes with the flow of the game, the children could simply tick off/colour in the relevant boxes on the record sheet to show which items they have bought and then enter the amounts at the end of the game. Encourage the children to work out their final totals on the record sheet before checking their answer with a calculator – again, using a pencil is advisable here. It is important to demonstrate to the children how the first two columns have subtotals which need to be carried over to the top of the next column in order to calculate the checkout total. Discuss the overall calculation process to make sure the children understand the vocabulary being used. If they make a mistake, can they see where they went wrong? (The subtotals will help them to break the addition down into stages.) Children could use toy money as a visual aid to their calculations.

GAME VARIATIONS

- A simpler version of this game is to take away the money element in order to turn it into a basic recording activity. As suggested above, the players can shade in/tick off the entries on the record sheet to indicate which items they have bought and then count the total number of items they have each bought at the end of the game. The player with the highest total wins.
- An element of realism can be introduced by playing the game in reverse. Give each player a starting amount of £20, and each time an item is purchased its cost is deducted from the total. The players' running totals can be recorded on an adapted version of the record sheet or on a piece of paper. A calculator can be used if necessary. Any player who spends more than £20 is out of the game, and the player with the most money left once he has passed the checkout is the winner.

EXTENSION

☆ Multiplying numbers to two decimal places in the context of money (N: 4a; MD: D)

This game can be adapted to incorporate multiplication by introducing the idea of bulk buying. In addition to the supermarket game board, trolley playing pieces, dice and shaker, a bag of single digit number cards is needed; and to keep score, each player needs a copy of record sheet 44. The game is played as above, but each time a player lands on a square they draw a single digit number card from the bag to find out the number of items they must buy. This number is recorded in the 'X' column. The name and price of the item is also recorded along with the price of 'X' number of items. If a player can work out the multiplication correctly without using a calculator, he gets a £1 bonus and places a tick in the bonus column next to that item. Once all of the players have passed the checkout, they can then work out the total amount of money they have spent, using a calculator if necessary. Point out that subtotal A (the total of the first column) needs to be carried over to the top of the second column in order to continue the addition. The total of £1 bonuses can be subtracted from the overall total at the end of the addition. The player who has spent the least money is the winner.

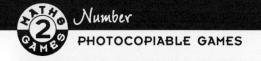

Number — PHOTOCOPIABLE GAMES — SCHOLASTIC PHOTOCOPIABLES — SUPERMARKET

HOW TO PLAY SUPERMARKET

For 2 to 4 players.

YOU NEED: a supermarket game board, a trolley playing piece and record sheet for each player, a dice and shaker, a calculator.

❶ Each player chooses a shopping trolley playing piece and places it at the entrance to the supermarket.

❷ Take it in turns to throw the dice and move your shopping trolley along the track.

❸ Each time you land on a square you must buy that item. Write down the price of that item on your record sheet. Make sure you write down the price correctly.

❹ Continue playing until all the players have been all the way round the supermarket and have passed out of the exit.

❺ Now add up the total amount you have spent in the supermarket. The player with the highest total is the winner.

SHOPPING TROLLEY PLAYING PIECES
Colour each playing piece a different colour (red, blue, green and yellow). Cut out, fold, stick and hold.

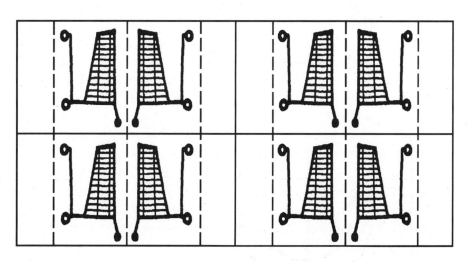

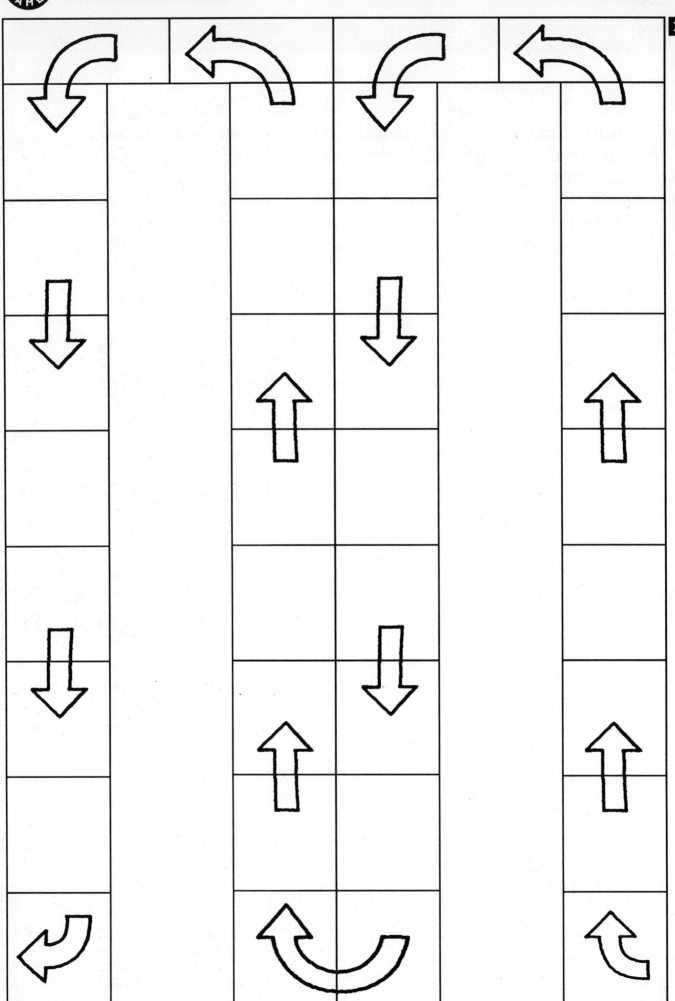

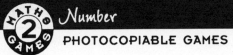

SUPERMARKET

	Freezer	Drinks and Sweets		Household Goods	Dairy and Meat	
98p	lollies	tea	£1.87	mugs	£1.40	butter	76p
£1.99	ice cream	coffee	£1.58	brushes	£1.25	cheese	£1.42
86p	carrots	lemonade	46p	nappies	£1.86	milk	55p
£1.52	broccoli	water	82p	tissues	71p	eggs	£1.10
£2.11	burgers	cola	53p	talc	£1.09	bacon	£1.51
£2.07	chicken	crisps	£1.19	shampoo	£1.34	sausages	97p
£1.88	pizza	chocolate	90p	toothpaste	82p	steak	£3.28
£1.64	chips	mints	75p	soap	33p	chops	£2.99

41

SUPERMARKET

Flour and Jam		Bakery		Tins		Fruit and Veg	
sugar	74p	loaf	59p	custard	38p	apples	36p
rice	93p	rolls	50p	meatballs	72p	oranges	42p
flour	96p	pitta	57p	sardines	43p	bananas	40p
cornflakes	£1.04	scones	79p	salmon	65p	lettuce	51p
marmalade	81p	doughnuts	44p	soup	31p	cucumber	33p
jam	70p	crumpets	63p	spaghetti	26p	tomatoes	49p
pears	52p	cakes	98p	beans	27p	potatoes	18p
peaches	47p	pies	85p	peas	24p	onions	25p

RECORD SHEET FOR SUPERMARKET

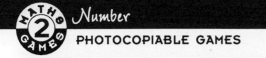 Name

apples	●	subtotal A (carried over)	●	subtotal B (carried over)	●
oranges	●	rolls	●	talc	●
bananas	●	loaf	●	tissues	●
lettuce	●	peaches	●	nappies	●
cucumber	●	pears	●	brushes	●
tomatoes	●	jam	●	mugs	●
potatoes	●	marmalade	●	tea	●
onions	●	cornflakes	●	coffee	●
peas	●	flour	●	lemonade	●
beans	●	rice	●	water	●
spaghetti	●	sugar	●	cola	●
soup	●	butter	●	crisps	●
salmon	●	cheese	●	chocolate	●
sardines	●	milk	●	mints	●
meatballs	●	eggs	●	chips	●
custard	●	bacon	●	pizza	●
pies	●	sausages	●	chicken	●
cakes	●	steak	●	burgers	●
doughnuts	●	chops	●	broccoli	●
crumpets	●	soap	●	carrots	●
scones	●	toothpaste	●	ice-cream	●
pitta	●	shampoo	●	lollies	●
subtotal A	●	subtotal B	●	checkout total	●

RECORD SHEET FOR SUPERMARKET (EXTENSION)

Name:

X	Item/price	£	✓	X	Item/price	£	✓
		•			subtotal A (carried over)	•	
		•				•	
		•				•	
		•				•	
		•				•	
		•				•	
		•				•	
		•				•	
		•				•	
		•				•	
		•				•	
		•				•	
		•				•	
		•				•	
		•			subtotal B	•	
		•			less bonus £'s	•	
	subtotal A	•			total	•	

MAKE A FIVER

TEACHING CONTENT

★ Using decimals in the context of money (N: 2b; RTN: C)
★ Developing mental methods of computation with whole numbers less than 1000 to solve problems (N: 3d, 4b; RTN: B)
★ Practising addition of one- and two-digit numbers (N: 3d; AS: C)
★ Using coins/notes to £5 worth or more (M: C)
★ Using practical resources as tools for exploring number structure (N:1b)

WHAT YOU NEED

PHOTOCOPIABLE SHEETS
Money meter (front) sheet 140, Money meter number wheels sheet 141, coin cards sheet 36, 'How to play' sheet 46, record sheet 47.

FOR CONSTRUCTION
Card, glue, scissors, 3 paper fasteners or card rivets.

FOR PLAYING
Money meter (preferably one for each player), coin cards, bag, 'How to play' sheet, record sheet and pencil, collection of coins (optional), calculator (optional).

PREPARATION

You will need to construct the Money meter from the Special section (pages 140 and 141). Ideally, there should be a meter for each player. Explain to the children how the meter works, making sure they understand which part of the meter to use for which coins. Show them that there are pictures on the face of the meter to remind them. You will also need to make up the coin cards (page 36) that go in the bag.

HOW TO PLAY

This is a game for two or more players. In turn each player takes a coin out of the bag and moves her Money meter to show the number of pence indicated by the coin. Players continue taking turns to pick coins out of the bag and add the amount of the coin drawn to their Money meter. After each draw, the coin is replaced in the bag. Play continues until players reach £5 or more. Players cannot stop below £5. As each player finishes, she fills in a strip on the record sheet. When all players have finished, they should work out their final positions. The player who makes closest to £5 is the winner.

TEACHER'S ROLE

This game is not as easy as it appears. Not only does it require the children to understand how the values of the coins relate to positions on the meter, it also requires the child to 'add on' from one window to another. If, for example, a child has 7p in the hundredths window, having drawn a 5p coin and then a 2p coin, and she then picks a 20p coin from the bag, how does she respond? Does she immediately move the tenths wheel to 2? Does she count on from the hundredths window, carrying the tens into the tenths window as she goes? Does she merely keep moving the hundredths wheel around? It may be helpful to have a collection of coins on hand, so that children who are having difficulty can check their calculations. A calculator is also useful as a checking tool for children who have grasped the concept of adding on tens and whole pounds.

Check that children have worked out their positions accurately on the record sheet.

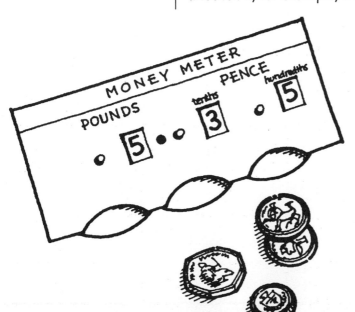

HOW TO PLAY MAKE A FIVER

For 2 or more players.

YOU NEED: Money meter (preferably one for each player), coin cards, bag, record sheet and pencil, collection of coins (optional), calculator (optional).

❶ Put the coin cards into the bag and shake the bag.

❷ In turn, each player takes a coin card out of the bag and moves his Money meter wheels to show the number of pence that the coin shows. After each go, put the coin card back in the bag.

❸ Players continue to pick coins out of the bag in turn, each time adding the number of pence drawn to the amount shown on their meter.

❹ Each player keeps playing until his meter shows £5 or more, then stops and writes his total on the record sheet.

For example, your meter might show £4.96. Then you draw a 50p coin from the bag. This takes you to £5.46. You put the coin back in the bag and write your total on the record sheet.

❺ When everyone else has finished, work out your final positions. The player nearest £5 wins.

☆ REMEMBER!

You must put your coin card back in the bag after each move.

You cannot stop playing until you have reached £5.00 or more. So if you have £4.99, you must still have another go!

RECORD SHEET FOR MAKE A FIVER

Name

£5.☐☐

I was ☐ out of ☐ players.

Name

£5.☐☐

I was ☐ out of ☐ players.

Name

£5.☐☐

I was ☐ out of ☐ players.

Name

£5.☐☐

I was ☐ out of ☐ players.

COIN HOPSCOTCH

WHAT YOU NEED

PHOTOCOPIABLE SHEETS
Money meter (front) sheet 140, Money meter number wheels sheet 141, coin cards sheet 36, Coin hopscotch game board sheet 50, 'How to play' sheet 49, record sheet 51.

FOR CONSTRUCTION
Card, glue, scissors, 3 paper fasteners or card rivets.

FOR PLAYING
Money meter, coin cards, bag, game board, 'How to play' sheet, record sheet and pencil, calculator.

TEACHING CONTENT

★ Using practical resources as tools for exploring number structure (N:1b)
★ Understanding multiplication as repeated addition (N: 3e; MD: B, C)
★ Practising addition with two decimal places using money (N: 2b, 4a; AS: D; M: B)
★ Using a calculator (N: 3g, h, 4a, c; IH: B)

PREPARATION

You will need to construct the Money meter from the Special section (pages 140 and 141). Explain to the children how the meter works, making sure they understand which part of the meter to use for which coins. Show them that there are pictures on the face of the meter to remind them. You will also need to make up the coin cards (page 36).

As the game is played by one player at a time, it can be fitted into spare moments and completed over a lengthy period of time. For this reason, it would be best to photocopy the game board on to card.

HOW TO PLAY

This is a game for two or more players, and the aim is to be the player with the most money at the end. Players play the game one at a time. The player shakes the bag of coin cards, takes one out and places it on top of the same coin on the Coin hopscotch board. She keeps doing this, making piles of coins whenever the same coin is picked repeatedly. The player stops when all the coins on the board have been covered. She then uses the Money meter to check how much she has in each section.

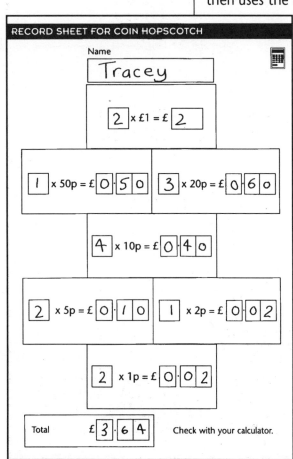

If there is one 50p coin, for example, she should show £0.50 for this section. If there is are three 20p coins, the tenths wheel is moved in twos until £0.60 is reached. These amounts are recorded on the record sheet. All the separate coin totals are added together on the Money meter. The total is then checked using a calculator. When all players have had a go, the player with the highest total wins.

The players can also use the Money meter *during* the game to keep a running total. Either way, the meter acts as a checking device.

TEACHER'S ROLE

The main emphasis in this game is on translating coin values into the correct decimal format. There is some multiplication of decimals, but this is on a very simple level. As the children are playing one at a time, observe them individually to see how well they understand the concept of multiplication by repeated addition and their ability to create the decimal layout on the Money meter. Some children may have difficulty with the 1p, 2p and 5p layouts, which require a nought in front of them below a total value of 10p. Discourage the use of the calculator except for the final addition and checking.

HOW TO PLAY COIN HOPSCOTCH

For 2 or more players.

YOU NEED: Money meter, coin cards, bag, game board, record sheet and pencil, calculator.

Players play the game one at a time, and the aim is to be the player with the most money at the end.

❶ Shake the bag of coin cards, take one out and place it on top of the same coin on the game board.

❷ Keep doing this, making piles of coins whenever you pick the same coin more than once.

❸ Stop when all the coins on the board have been covered.

❹ Then use the Money meter to work how much you have for each coin value.

So, if you have one 20p coin, move the meter to £0.20 and write that amount on the record sheet. If there is more than one coin in a section, say three 2p coins, add them together – £0.02 + £0.02 + £0.02 = £0.06.

❺ Record each section total on the record sheet and then use the Money Meter to work out the grand total. Check your answer with a calculator.

❻ When all players have had a go, the player with the highest total wins.

COIN HOPSCOTCH GAME BOARD

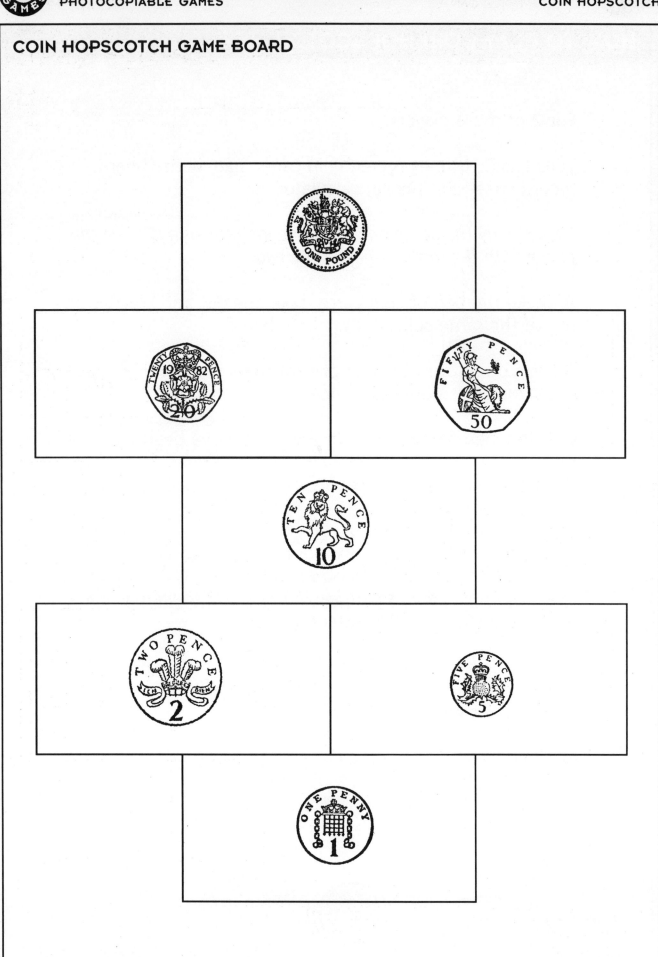

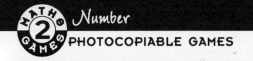 **SCHOLASTIC PHOTOCOPIABLES**

COIN HOPSCOTCH

RECORD SHEET FOR COIN HOPSCOTCH

Name

☐ × £1 = £ ☐

☐ × 50p = £ ☐ . ☐☐   ☐ × 20p = £ ☐ . ☐☐

☐ × 10p = £ ☐ . ☐☐

☐ × 5p = £ ☐ . ☐☐   ☐ × 2p = £ ☐ . ☐☐

☐ × 1p = £ ☐ . ☐☐

Total   £ ☐ . ☐☐   Check with your calculator.

BOX OFFICE

WHAT YOU NEED

PHOTOCOPIABLE SHEETS
Cinema seats sheet 31, spectator playing pieces sheet 32, tickets sheet 55, 'How to play' sheet 54, record sheets 56 and 57 (extension).

FOR CONSTRUCTION
Card, scissors, glue, adhesive tape, sticky labels, coloured pens or pencils, a dice or building block.

FOR PLAYING
A cinema game board, a set of playing pieces in a different colour for each player (red, blue, green and yellow), a set of priced tickets for the cinema seats, record sheet, 'How to play' sheet, a colour dice and shaker.

TEACHING CONTENT

★ Using decimals to two decimal places in the context of money (N: 2b; RTN: C; AS: D)
★ Understanding multiplication as repeated addition (N: 3e; MD: D)
★ Using a calculator (N: 1b; RTN: C)

PREPARATION

Photocopy sheets 31, 32 and 55 on to card. A piece of card 40cm × 25cm is also needed to serve as the base for the cinema. Cut up sheet 32 to make individual spectator playing pieces and fold as indicated. Cut up sheet 55 to make the tickets for the cinema seats. See page 37 for construction notes on how to build the cinema. A dice needs to be made to represent the three rows of the cinema. This can be made by sticking labels on to the sides of a building block or standard dice and labelling opposite faces with the letters A, B and C.

HOW TO PLAY

This is a game for four players. Each player chooses one of the coloured sets (red, blue, green or yellow) and collects all of the audience playing pieces in that colour. Only one 'cinema' game board is needed to play this game. The players take turns to throw the dice in order to decide in which row (A, B or C) they can place one of their spectators. It is their decision which seat number to occupy. When a player has placed the spectator on the seat in the cinema, she can then collect the ticket for that seat from the 'box office'. Play continues until all of the seats are taken. The players then count up how many seats they have in each row and write in these numbers on the record sheet. They can then work out the total price of their seats in each row, and the total prices of all of the seats they have occupied in the cinema. The player with the highest overall total is the winner.

TEACHER'S ROLE

Make sure that the children understand the principles behind this game: each seat is 'labelled' by 'row' and 'number', there is one ticket per seat and the seats in different rows have different prices. During the game, ask questions to develop the children's mathematical awareness of their progress. How many seats in Row A do you have? How much are these seats worth? Can the children appreciate that though addition and multiplication are different processes, they can be used to represent the same calculation? For example: £1.25 + £1.25 + £1.25 = £3.75 and 3 × £1.25 = £3.75. Help the children to develop strategies for addition and multiplication: two 25s make 50, so four 25s make 100, which can then be added to the whole numbers (in this case £s). Children could use toy money as a visual aid to working out their totals; and if necessary, calculators can be used to check/calculate the totals. It may be best if children use pencil rather than pen to record their initial calculations before checking with the calculator, in case of error. Change the roles of the players: if they play the part of the cinema manager, how much money will they make from each full row? How much from a full house?

This could lead on to work on subtraction and fractions. How much would you make if only half of the seats in each row were taken? If $9/10$ of the seats were full? (And so on.)

GAME VARIATION

The game can be adapted according to the children's ability by changing the prices of the tickets – either to more simple numbers (ending in 20, 50 or 00) or to more difficult ones (ending in 30, 40, 60, 70, 80 or 90). The 'reserved' cards can also be placed at the start of the game to make the game shorter.

EXTENSIONS

★ Understanding and calculating averages (HD: 2c; IH: E)

This game can be extended to introduce the concept of averages. At the end of the game, each of the players can work out the average price of the seats they have bought by dividing their overall total by their number of seats. Are their finishing positions reflected in the average price of their seats? Can they see why this might be so? Look at the average seat prices for each row. Why is this average total different from their individual average totals? If you wish, you could amend the seat prices to vary the totals, perhaps with a reduction of 50p for all seats and lower-priced seats for senior citizens and children (obviously the players will need to look at the 'characters' on their spectator playing pieces). The winner is the player with the lowest average seat cost.

★ Calculating percentages (N: 2c; FPR: E)
★ Using a calculator for calculations involving numbers to two decimal places (N: 2b; MD: E)

By introducing the idea of a discount for group bookings, this activity can also be adapted for work on percentages. The children will, of course, need some familiarity with percentages before attempting this type of work. Play the game as above, and at the end the children can work out the percentage discount for each row, recording their calculations on the record sheets. The discount will depend on the number of seats they have bought – three to five seats receives a discount of 6%, six to eight 8%, nine to eleven 10%, twelve to fourteen 15%, fifteen and over 18%. The children can use the record sheet to work out the discounted price for each of their rows and then calculate their overall saving. This provides a good opportunity for calculator practice. Ask questions as the children calculate their percentages, to develop their awareness of the process they are using. Look at how percentages can be calculated without using the '%' button on the calculator, so that they understand how percentages work. How is a percentage written as a fraction? Show the relationship between the arithmetical process and the procedure of working this out on a calculator, as shown on the left. Watch to see which children understand the mathematical process, which ones are merely following a formula but do not understand 'why' the process works, and which ones get lost within the steps of the calculation. Introducing other percentage discounts can help to check that children understand the overall process.

arithmetical

$$\frac{\text{price} \times \square}{100} = \text{new price}$$

calculator

price × □ ÷ 100 = new price

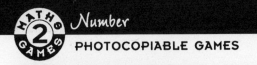

HOW TO PLAY BOX OFFICE

For 4 players.

YOU NEED: a cinema game board, a complete set of spectator playing pieces, a complete set of tickets, an A, B, C dice and shaker, a calculator, pencils, coloured crayons, rubbers, a record sheet for each player.

❶ Each player chooses a colour (red, blue, green or yellow) and collects that set of spectator playing pieces.

❷ Take turns to throw the dice. The letter you throw tells you in which row of the cinema you can place one of your spectator playing pieces. You can choose the seat number yourself.

❸ Collect a ticket from the pile to show you have bought that seat.

So: if you are blue and you throw 'A', you can place one of your blue spectators on any empty seat in row 'A' and collect a ticket for row 'A' with the seat number you have chosen to show that you have bought the seat.

❹ Continue playing until all of the seats in the cinema are taken.

❺ Now fill in the record sheet. Count up the number of seats you have bought in each row. Write in these numbers, then multiply the cost of the seats in each row by the number of seats you have bought in that row. Fill in your totals.

*So: if you have bought 4 seats in row 'A',
4 × £1.75 = £7.00*

❻ Add up your totals to see how much money you have spent altogether. The player with the highest total is the winner.

TICKETS FOR BOX OFFICE
Cut up this sheet to make individual tickets.

ROW A SEAT 1 £1.75	ROW A SEAT 2 £1.75	ROW A SEAT 3 £1.75

| ROW A SEAT 4 £1.75 | ROW A SEAT 5 £1.75 | ROW A SEAT 6 £1.75 | ROW A SEAT 7 £1.75 | ROW A SEAT 8 £1.75 | ROW A SEAT 9 £1.75 | ROW A SEAT 10 £1.75 | ROW B SEAT 1 £1.50 | ROW B SEAT 2 £1.50 |

| ROW B SEAT 3 £1.50 | ROW B SEAT 4 £1.50 | ROW B SEAT 5 £1.50 | ROW B SEAT 6 £1.50 | ROW B SEAT 7 £1.50 | ROW B SEAT 8 £1.50 | ROW B SEAT 9 £1.50 | ROW B SEAT 10 £1.50 | ROW C SEAT 1 £1.25 |

| ROW C SEAT 2 £1.25 | ROW C SEAT 3 £1.25 | ROW C SEAT 4 £1.25 | ROW C SEAT 5 £1.25 | ROW C SEAT 6 £1.25 | ROW C SEAT 7 £1.25 | ROW C SEAT 8 £1.25 | ROW C SEAT 9 £1.25 | ROW C SEAT 10 £1.25 |

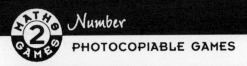

SCHOLASTIC PHOTOCOPIABLES

BOX OFFICE

RECORD SHEET FOR BOX OFFICE

Name						colour	1st	2nd	3rd	4th
	row	seats		cost						
	A		x £1.75	£		●				
	B		x £1.50	£		●				
	C		x £1.25	£		●				
			total	£		●				

Name						colour	1st	2nd	3rd	4th
	row	seats		cost						
	A		x £1.75	£		●				
	B		x £1.50	£		●				
	C		x £1.25	£		●				
			total	£		●				

Name						colour	1st	2nd	3rd	4th
	row	seats		cost						
	A		x £1.75	£		●				
	B		x £1.50	£		●				
	C		x £1.25	£		●				
			total	£		●				

Name						colour	1st	2nd	3rd	4th
	row	seats		cost						
	A		x £1.75	£		●				
	B		x £1.50	£		●				
	C		x £1.25	£		●				
			total	£		●				

SCHOLASTIC PHOTOCOPIABLES
BOX OFFICE

RECORD SHEET FOR BOX OFFICE (EXTENSION)

Name					colour	1st	2nd	3rd	4th
row	seats	cost without discount		party cost					
A		£ •		£ •		number of seats			
B		£ •		£ •		discount			
C		£ •		£ •		total saved			
	total	£ •		£ •		£ •			

Name					colour	1st	2nd	3rd	4th
row	seats	cost without discount		party cost					
A		£ •		£ •		number of seats			
B		£ •		£ •		discount			
C		£ •		£ •		total saved			
	total	£ •		£ •		£ •			

Name					colour	1st	2nd	3rd	4th
row	seats	cost without discount		party cost					
A		£ •		£ •		number of seats			
B		£ •		£ •		discount			
C		£ •		£ •		total saved			
	total	£ •		£ •		£ •			

Name					colour	1st	2nd	3rd	4th
row	seats	cost without discount		party cost					
A		£ •		£ •		number of seats			
B		£ •		£ •		discount			
C		£ •		£ •		total saved			
	total	£ •		£ •		£ •			

CITY TRAFFIC

TEACHING CONTENT

★ Collecting, organising, displaying and interpreting data (HD: 2a, b; IH: B, C)

PREPARATION

Assembling the game: The game board is made by photocopying sheet 60 twice and and then cutting off the column of vehicles on one copy. Mount the sheets on to thick card, with the second sheet butted up to the first to make a 6 × 6 block graph (as shown below). Make the large and small playing cards by photocopying sheet 61 twice (preferably directly on to card, or mount on to card after copying) and cutting it up to make individual cards. Enhance the appearance and durability of the game by colouring and laminating both board and playing cards.

Introducing the game: Ideally, the group should have had the real experience of conducting a simple traffic survey, noting the types and numbers of vehicles passing a set point within a limited period of time. Discuss why surveys and censuses are carried out.

HOW TO PLAY

This game for six players simulates a traffic survey and uses a board that represents a block graph. The aim is to collect small cards representing single vehicles and exchange them for a larger pictogram which stands for a set number of 10. Each player chooses one of the six vehicles to collect. In turn, each player then throws the dice and collects that number of small cards for his vehicle. When a throw takes the player to 10 or more, the player exchanges ten small cards for one large one which is then placed on the board in the correct column. Any remaining small cards are kept by the player. So, if a player has collected 9 small cards and throws a 5 on his next throw, this means a total of 14 vehicles. He can therefore put 1 large vehicle card on the board (representing 10) and keep 4 small ones. The 10 small cards are then returned to the tray. The first player to place all 6 of the large cards on the board is the winner.

TEACHER'S ROLE

Central to this game is the idea that the large pictogram cards represent 10 vehicles. During play, observe whether children have grasped this concept and are easily able to see that, for instance, a total of 15 means 1 large card and 5 small ones. After the game, use the finished board to discuss the data it shows. While one vehicle, the winning one, will have 6 large pictograms, the others will have a variety of large and small cards. Ask the children to add their small cards to the grid and to work out how many of each vehicle type are represented. How many vehicles altogether? Can you use a calculator to find out? Vary the language in which you phrase your questions. For instance: How many more, or fewer, buses are there than motorbikes? What is the difference between the numbers of cars and lorries? Use the data to instigate other sorts of mathematical problem solving. For example, if the survey took 15 minutes, what was the hourly rate of vehicles passing?

WHAT YOU NEED

PHOTOCOPIABLE SHEETS
Game board sheet 60, playing cards sheet 61, 'How to play' sheet 59.

FOR CONSTRUCTION
Thick card 28cm × 24cm, scissors, glue, coloured felt-tipped pens (optional), clear plastic adhesive film (optional).

FOR PLAYING
Game board, 'How to play' sheet, large and small playing cards, a dice and shaker, 2 trays for playing cards.

HOW TO PLAY CITY TRAFFIC

For 6 players.

YOU NEED: a game board, large and small playing cards, a dice and shaker, 2 trays for the playing cards.

❶ Place the large cards in one tray and the small cards in the other. Put the trays where everyone can reach them.

❷ Choose which vehicle each of you will collect.

❸ Take it in turns to throw the dice and collect that number of small cards for your vehicle.

❹ When a throw takes you to 10 or more, you can exchange 10 small cards for 1 large one which you place on the board in the column for the vehicle you have chosen. Keep any remaining small cards.

So, if you have collected 9 small cards and throw a 5 on your next throw, this means you have a total of 14 vehicles. You can therefore put 1 large vehicle card on the board (representing 10) and keep 4 small ones.

❺ The first player to place all six of his large cards on the board is the winner.

GAME BOARD FOR CITY TRAFFIC
See page 58 for construction.

Car			
Bicycle			
Lorry			
Bus			
Motorbike			
Van			

Number
PHOTOCOPIABLE GAMES

SCHOLASTIC PHOTOCOPIABLES

CITY TRAFFIC

PLAYING CARDS FOR CITY TRAFFIC
Cut up this sheet to make individual cards.

61

SQUARE MEAL

TEACHING CONTENT

★ Working with numbers to two decimal places in the context of money (N: 2b; RTN: C, D)
★ Practising addition and subtraction to solve problems involving money (N: 3c; AS: C; M: C, D)
★ Using a calculator (N: 3h, 4a; RTN: C)

PREPARATION

Assembling the game: Copy photocopiable sheets 66 and 67 directly on to card (or mount on to card after copying). To enhance the visual impact, colour in the items of food and laminate before cutting them up to make 24 individual playing cards. As the teacher sets the objective for each game played (see 'Teacher's role' below), you will need to determine this beforehand. If you wish to adjust the prices on the menu sheet, make a copy of photocopiable sheet 65 and adapt it before giving it to the players. The group will also need a copy of the record sheet on photocopiable sheet 68. The Money meter (from the Special section, photocopiable sheets 140 and 141) would be a useful tool for this game.

Introducing the game: The context of buying a meal will be familiar to most children. Explain that the aim of the game is to buy a complete meal: a full plate of main course items, plus a drink and a dessert. Go through the menu sheet with them to ensure that everyone knows what the items are. Ask: if you could choose any of the items on the menu, which would you choose? Does that represent a healthy meal? Then tell the children the particular goal you have decided for the game.

HOW TO PLAY

This is a game for two to four players, the mathematical objective of which is set by the teacher before each game begins. The playing cards are spread out, face up in front of the players. Players take it in turns to throw the dice, and can choose any food with the same number. Which food they choose will depend on the object of the game. If, for instance,

WHAT YOU NEED

PHOTOCOPIABLE SHEETS
Square meal playing cards sheets 66 and 67, 'How to play' sheet 64, Menu price list sheet 65, record sheet 68, Money meter sheets 140 and 141 (optional).

FOR CONSTRUCTION
Card, coloured pencils or felt-tipped pens (optional), glue, clear adhesive plastic, scissors, three paper fasteners (optional).

FOR PLAYING
A set of 24 Square meal playing cards, 'How to play' sheet, menu price list, record sheet, dice and shaker, calculator, Money meter (optional).

the object of the game is to obtain the cheapest meal, players will obviously want to pick the cheapest of each type of food. So if the first player throws a 3, she will opt for noodles which are the cheapest item in that food section. (Obviously this may not be the case if you choose to adapt the price list.) Once a player has chosen a card, she keeps it and it is the next player's turn. If a player throws a number for which she already has a meal item, she cannot go and play moves on to the next player. Play continues until everyone has 'bought' a complete meal using all six numbers. Then everyone records their purchased meals on the record sheet (either by drawing the items or by writing their names and prices), and works out how much each meal has cost using a calculator and/or the Money meter (from the Special section, photocopiable sheets 140 and 141). The winner is the player who has achieved, or come closest to achieving, the goal set by the teacher.

TEACHER'S ROLE

As indicated above, although the rules themselves remain the same (i.e. each player has to 'buy' a complete meal), the goals for this game can be varied to practise a range of mathematical skills, and should be set by the teacher beforehand. The simplest game, and one meant to familiarise the players with the cards rather than achieve a mathematical objective, is to see who gets the first complete meal. Then who gets the cheapest/ dearest meal? Who gets the meal closest to a target amount, say £3 or £5? Who gets the most change from £5 or £10? In addition, the menu price list can be adapted easily. The mixed pence and pound prices could be changed to all pence or all pound prices. Or prices could be limited to a certain number range, and so on.

In recording and totalling their meal items, players will need to have an understanding of how pence convert to decimal pounds in order to use the calculator. The Money meter (from the Special section), which allows children to experiment with this concept, would be helpful. Children should be developing the skill of calculating ongoing cost, and be able to see that the 'bill' for their meal is a type of addition problem.

HOW TO PLAY SQUARE MEAL

For 2 to 4 players.

YOU NEED: a set of 24 Square meal playing cards, a menu price list, a record sheet, a dice and shaker, pencils, a calculator, a Money meter (optional).

❶ Ask your teacher what players in your group have to do to win.

❷ Spread the playing cards out, face up, on the table and put the menu with its list of prices where everyone can see it. Decide on your playing order.

❸ In turn, each player throws the dice and can choose any food card with the same number. Which food you choose depends on the object of the game.

So, if the object of the game is to get the cheapest meal, you will obviously want to pick the cheapest of each type of food.

❹ Once you have chosen a card, you keep it and it is the next player's turn.

❺ Play continues until everyone has 'bought' a complete meal, using all six numbers.

❻ Then everyone records their purchased meals on the record sheet, and works out how much each meal has cost using a calculator or the Money meter or both.

❼ The winner is the player who has achieved, or come closest to achieving, the goal set by the teacher.

☆ REMEMBER!

If you throw a number for which you already have a meal item, you cannot go and play moves on to the next player.

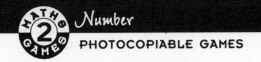

SQUARE MEAL PLAYING CARDS

SQUARE MEAL PLAYING CARDS

RECORD SHEET FOR SQUARE MEAL

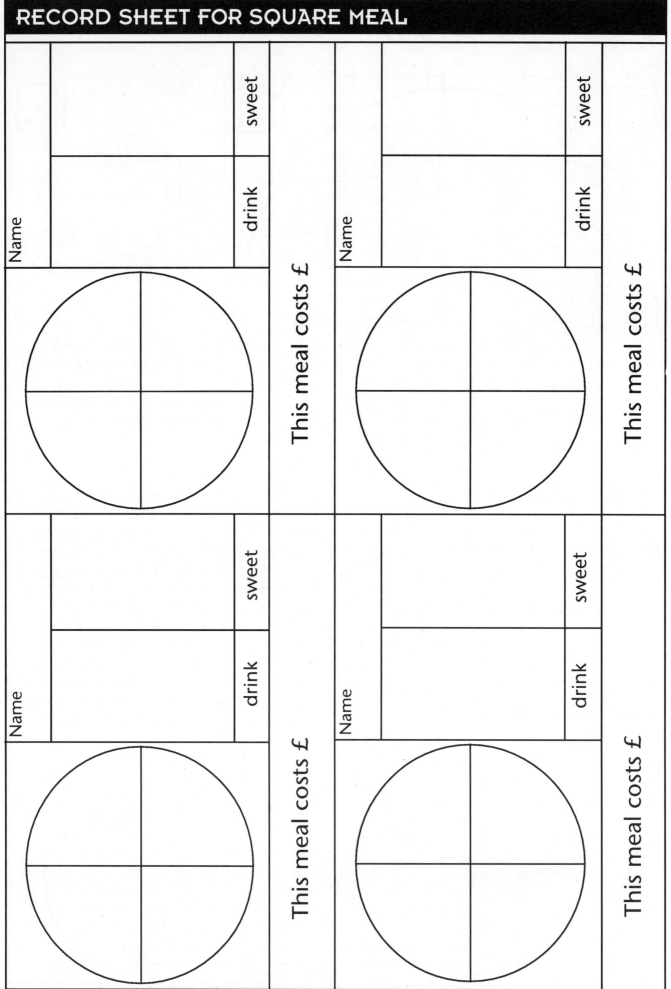

WHAT'S THE DIFFERENCE?

WHAT YOU NEED

PHOTOCOPIABLE SHEETS
Number meter sheet 144, 'How to play' sheet 71, record sheet 72.

FOR CONSTRUCTION
Card, glue, scissors, 4 paper fasteners or card rivets.

FOR PLAYING
Number meter, 'How to play' sheet, record sheet, dice and shaker, calculator, pencils.

TEACHING CONTENT

★ Reading, writing and ordering whole numbers up to 10 000 to develop understanding of place value (N: 2a; RTN: C)
★ Introducing the concept of symbols used for missing numbers or unknown numbers (N: 3a; FE: B)
★ Developing an understanding of the inverse relationship between addition and subtraction (N: 3f; AS: D)
★ Practising subtraction with 4-digit numbers using a calculator (N: 3h, 4a, c; AS: D)

PREPARATION

You will need to construct the Number meter from the Special section (page 144). Ideally, there should be one meter for each player. Explain to the children how the meter works. It's rather like an old-fashioned gas meter, and can demonstrate numbers from 0000 to 9999. Show them how the squares on the record sheet relate to the positions of the numbers on the meter.

HOW TO PLAY

This is a game for two or more players. Give each player a Number meter set to 0000 (or one meter can be passed from player to player). The players take it in turns to create two 4-digit numbers and then find the difference between them. To create each number, the player has two throws of the dice for each wheel on the Number meter. Starting with the units, he throws the dice and moves the ones wheel by the number indicated. He throws again and moves the wheel on by the number indicated. So if the first throw is 6 and the second 5, the ones wheel would end up at 1. (In this game there is no adding on from wheel to wheel.) The same is done for the tens, hundreds and thousands wheels. When the first number has been created, it is written on the record sheet. The same is done for the second number. The player then has to calculate the difference using a calculator and write the answer on the record sheet. Play passes to the next player. At the end, the player with the largest difference is the winner.

TEACHER'S ROLE

Besides creating the two 4-digit numbers, the players are required to subtract one from the other to find the difference. Emphasise the word 'difference'. Make sure the children understand that 'difference' in mathematical terms means a numerical value, the number that has to be added to the smaller number to get the larger. It does not refer to any physical description of the numerals! They will need to understand the inverse relationship of addition and subtraction in order to know that they have to subtract the smaller number from the larger, even if the larger number is the second one they have created. Observe as they input the calculation, to determine whether they have grasped this.

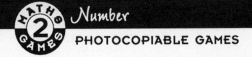

WHAT'S THE DIFFERENCE?

GAME VARIATIONS

The Number meter can be adapted to show just hundreds, tens and units (or even just tens and units) and the game adapted accordingly.

EXTENSION

★ Developing further understanding and use of the relationship between addition and subtraction, including inverses (N: 3f; PS: E)
★ Introducing mathematical vocabulary (UA: 3a)
★ Exploring missing numbers (N: 3a; PS: D)

As in the previous game, require the children to make two numbers – this time the difference and either the subtrahend (the number to be subtracted) or the minuend (the number from which another is to be subtracted). If the subtrahend and difference are chosen, they would be added to make the minuend; if the minuend and difference are chosen, the difference is subtracted from the minuend to find the subtrahend. The winner still remains the one with the largest answer. How much you want to use the above terminology depends on the ability of the children. Some children are quite happy with what appear to be complicated words and expressions, and frequently surprise adults by their comprehending use of them.

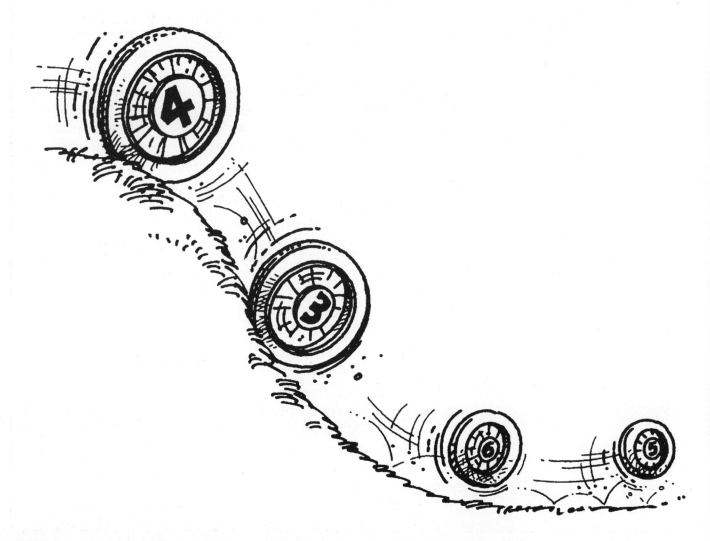

HOW TO PLAY WHAT'S THE DIFFERENCE?

For 2 or more players.

YOU NEED: Number meter, record sheet 72, dice and shaker, calculator, pencils.

❶ Set the Number meter to 0000.

❷ Take it in turns to create two 4-digit numbers each and then find the difference between them. To create each number, throw the dice twice for each wheel on the Number meter.

Start with the units. Throw the dice and move the units wheel the number indicated. Throw again and move the wheel on by the number indicated. So if your first throw is 6 and the second 5, the units wheel would end up at 1. (In this game there is no adding on from wheel to wheel.)

Do the same for the tens, hundreds and thousands wheels.

❸ When your first number has been created, write it on the record sheet.

❹ Repeat the procedure for the second number.

❺ Calculate the difference between the two numbers using a calculator and write the answer on the record sheet.

❻ Now it is the next player's turn.

❼ When everyone has had a go, the player with the largest difference is the winner.

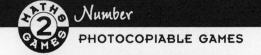

RECORD SHEET FOR WHAT'S THE DIFFERENCE?

Name

1st number

2nd number

Difference

Name

1st number

2nd number

Difference

Name

1st number

2nd number

Difference

Name

1st number

2nd number

Difference

NOUGHTY

WHAT YOU NEED

PHOTOCOPIABLE SHEETS
Noughty meter sheet 143, 'How to play' sheet 75, record/spinner sheet 76, 1 to 9 number cards sheet 34.

FOR CONSTRUCTION
Card, glue, scissors, matchstick, 1 paper fastener or card rivet.

FOR PLAYING
Noughty meter, 'How to play' sheet, record sheet, spinner, bag with two sets of 1 to 9 number cards, two pencils, a calculator.

TEACHING CONTENT

★ Developing understanding of place value and the importance of nought in determining numerical value (N: 2a; RTN: B)
★ Using symbols to represent unknown numbers and operations (N: 3a; FE: B)
★ Extending mental methods of computation involving all four operations (N: 3d; AS: C; MD: C, D)
★ Checking results using a calculator (N: 1b, 4a, c; IH: B)

PREPARATION

You will need to construct the Noughty meter from the Special section (page 143). Explain to the children how the meter works, making sure they understand that the strips are used to indicate the hundreds and tens numbers and the wheel is used to indicate the operation sign. Show them how the shapes on the meter relate to the shapes on the record sheet. You will also need to make up two sets of 1 to 9 number cards (page 34) to go in the bag.

HOW TO PLAY

This is a game for two teams of four players each. Team A starts. The first player takes a number card from the bag and moves the hundreds slide on the meter to that number. She then takes another number card from the bag and moves the tens slide to that number. The number cards are then put back into the bag. The player spins the sign spinner and moves the sign wheel on the meter to the appropriate sign. The player has now created a number statement, which she writes on to the game record sheet for Team A. For example:

$$300 \div 40 =$$

Now the team *as a whole* works out the answer mentally (reaching a consensus through discussion), and one team member writes it *in pencil* on the record sheet. They then check the answer with a calculator and put a tick (for a correct answer) or a cross (for a wrong answer) in the calculator column. If the answer is wrong, it should be rubbed out and the correct answer written in.

Now it is the turn of Team B. When every player on each team has made a number statement and the answers have been worked out, the teams calculate their totals. The team with the highest total wins. If you want to reward accurate mental calculation, give each team five bonus points for each tick in the calculator column.

TEACHER'S ROLE

The importance of nought in determining numerical value is made explicit through this game. Using the meter, the four operations can be shown at work on the 'noughty' numbers. The players have to work out the answers mentally, and this is supported by making the game a team effort with collaboration. However, the game can easily be adapted for play by two individuals.

During the game, observe the players' level of understanding; and afterwards, ask questions which lead children to make conclusions and rules about adding, subtracting, multiplying and dividing numbers ending in one nought or two noughts. For example: When we add a number ending in two noughts to one ending in one nought, how many noughts are there in the answer? (*One.*) Try several examples. Is it always one? What happens when we multiply a number ending in two noughts by one ending in one nought? How many noughts are in the answer? Try several examples. Is it always three?

GAME VARIATION

If you want the children to concentrate on one operation only, the sign wheel on the meter can be temporarily fixed on one sign with a strip of sticky tape, and the use of the sign spinner can be omitted.

HOW TO PLAY NOUGHTY

For 2 teams of 4 players each.

YOU NEED: Noughty meter, record sheet, spinner, bag with two sets of 1 to 9 number cards, two pencils, calculator.

❶ Team A starts. The first player takes a number card from the bag and moves the hundreds slide on the meter to that number.

❷ She then takes another number card from the bag and moves the tens slide to that number. The number cards are then put back into the bag.

❸ The player spins the sign spinner and moves the sign wheel on the meter to the appropriate sign, making a number statement which she writes onto the game record sheet for Team A.
For example:

$$3\ 0\ 0 \quad \div \quad 4\ 0 \quad =$$

❹ Now the team *as a whole* works out the answer mentally (reaching an agreement through discussion). One team member then writes it in *in pencil* on the record sheet.

❺ Team A then checks the answer with a calculator and puts a tick (for a correct answer) or a cross (for a wrong answer) in the calculator column. If the answer is wrong, it should be rubbed out and the correct answer written in.

❻ Now it is the turn of Team B. When every player on each team has made a number statement and the answers have been worked out, the teams calculate their totals. The team with the highest total wins.

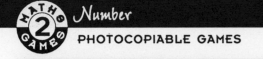

SCHOLASTIC PHOTOCOPIABLES

NOUGHTY

RECORD SHEET FOR NOUGHTY

Team A

☐ 00 △ ☐ 0 = ☐☐
☐ 00 △ ☐ 0 = ☐☐
☐ 00 △ ☐ 0 = ☐☐
☐ 00 △ ☐ 0 = ☐☐

Total ☐

✓
✗

Team B

☐ 00 △ ☐ 0 = ☐☐
☐ 00 △ ☐ 0 = ☐☐
☐ 00 △ ☐ 0 = ☐☐
☐ 00 △ ☐ 0 = ☐☐

Total ☐

✓
✗

The winning team was Team ☐A☐ ☐B☐

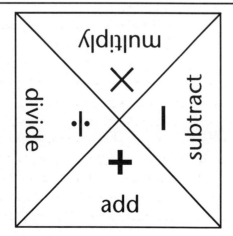

SIGN SPINNER
Cut out and mount on to card.
Push a matchstick through the centre.

SKYLINE

TEACHING CONTENT
★ Extending understanding of the number system to decimals up to two places (N: 2b; RTN: C)
★ Understanding fractions and using them in context to describe and compare proportions of a whole (N: 2c; FPR: C)

WHAT YOU NEED
PHOTOCOPIABLE SHEETS
Decimal meter (front) sheet 142, Decimal meter number wheels sheet 141, 'How to play' sheet 79, record sheet 80.
FOR CONSTRUCTION
Card, glue, scissors, 3 paper fasteners or card rivets.
FOR PLAYING
Decimal meter, 'How to play' sheet, record sheet, dice and shaker, coloured pencils.

PREPARATION
You will need to construct the Decimal meter from the Special section (pages 141 and 142). Explain to the children how the meter works. Show them the blocks on the face of the meter which indicate the relative values of the number positions: 1 in the hundredths position means 1/100 of a whole number; 1 in the tenths position means 1/10 of a whole number. 10 of the small squares under the hundredths window is the same as 1 row under the tenths window. And 10 rows under the tenths window is the same as the whole block under the whole ones window.

Now introduce the children to the concept of a city skyline. If you can find one, show them a picture of a skyline at night and see if they can see how it looks like a bar graph. Let them have a copy of the game record sheet, and explain that they are going to play a game to see who can rent out the most flats in the building on 100th Street, who can buy the most floors in the office block on 10th Avenue and who can build the tallest skyscraper on Whole Boulevard.

HOW TO PLAY
This is a game for two or more players. As each player completes the game individually, it can be done at odd moments of the day and extended over several days, with children coming together to see who has won at the end.

Each player is given the Decimal meter set to 0.00. Starting with the hundredths window, the player has two throws of the dice for each window on the Decimal meter. After each throw, he moves the number wheel the number of places shown on the dice.

For example, if he is working on the hundredths window and his first dice throw shows 5, he moves the hundredths wheel around to 5. He then throws again. If the number on the dice is 3, he moves the wheel around to 8. If, however, the second dice throw is a 6, he moves the wheel around through 0 to 1.

The player does the same for the tenths and whole ones windows. He then writes his final number on his record sheet, and colours in the appropriate blocks for each position (see overleaf).

When all the players have had a go, there are three possible winners (or chances of winning): the player who has rented the most flats in the building on 100th Street, the player who has bought the most floors in the office block on 10th Avenue and the player who has built the tallest skyscraper on Whole Boulevard.

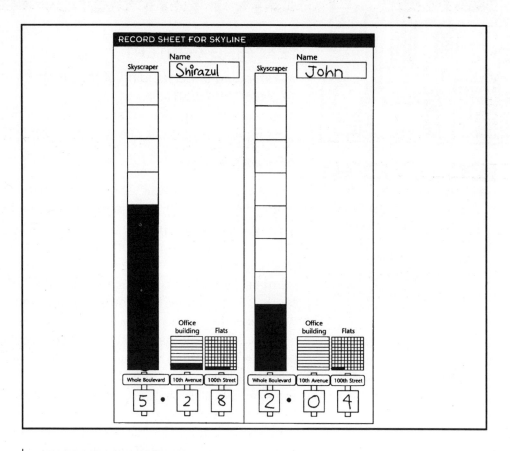

TEACHER'S ROLE

One of the problems with digits, when expressing decimal value, is that they all look the same. The child will know that 2 is less than 5, but what does she make of .2 or .02? To some extent, decimals mask the fractional meaning of the numbers; so if we can help children to see .2 as 2 tenths and .02 as 2 hundredths, we may further their understanding of decimal numbers. The Decimal meter and this game are designed to show decimals as fractions of a whole, and thus to bridge the conceptual gap between digital and fractional representation.

After the game, get the children to practise using the Decimal meter. Who can show me 5 hundredths on the meter? How would we write it? *(0.05)* Do we need the nought at the beginning? *(It helps to show there are no whole numbers and makes the number easier to read.)* Who can show me 5 tenths on the meter? How would we write it? *(0.50)* Do we need the nought at the end? How would we show 5 whole ones only? *(5.00)* Do we need the noughts after the decimal point? Lead the children to make some general conclusions.

EXTENSION

★ Developing understanding of addition involving two decimal places (N: 3d, g; AS: D)

Instead of treating each wheel individually, the players could add on the dice throws from one window to the next. So, if the first dice throw for the hundredths window is 5 and the second is 6, 1 is recorded in the hundredths window and 1 in the tenths window. The next pair of throws for the tenths window begins, therefore, at 1 rather than 0.

HOW TO PLAY SKYLINE

For 2 or more players.

YOU NEED: Decimal meter, record sheet, dice and shaker, coloured pencils.

The aim of the game is to be the player with the highest number in any of the three windows of the Decimal meter.

❶ Each player in turn is given the Decimal meter and sets it to 0.00.

❷ Starting with the hundredths window, throw the dice twice for each window on the Decimal meter. After each throw, move the number wheel the total number of places shown on the dice.

For example, if you are working on the hundredths window and your first dice throw shows 5, move the hundredths wheel around to 5. Then throw again. If the number on the dice is 3, move the wheel around to 8. If, however, the second dice throw is a 6, move the wheel around through 0 to 1.

❸ Do the same for the tenths and whole ones windows.

❹ Then write your final number on the record sheet and colour in the appropriate blocks for each position.

❺ When all the players have had a go, there are three chances of winning: the player who has rented the most flats in the building on 100th Street (the highest number in the hundredths position), the player who has bought the most floors in the office block on 10th Avenue (the highest number in the tenths position) and the player who has built the tallest skyscraper on Whole Boulevard (the highest number in the whole ones position).

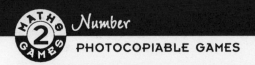

RECORD SHEET FOR SKYLINE

Name

Skyscraper

Office building   Flats

Whole Boulevard | 10th Avenue | 100th Street

Name

Skyscraper

Office building   Flats

Whole Boulevard | 10th Avenue | 100th Street

100 SQUARES OR SEQUENCES

TEACHING CONTENT
★ Exploring and explaining number patterns and sequences (N: 3a; PS: B)
★ Developing a range of mental methods for using known facts to find those which they cannot recall (N: 3c; FE: B, C)

PREPARATION
You will need one set of 1 to 9 and one set of 10 to 99 number cards (photocopiable sheets 34 and 35), plus an additional 100 card. You could, for this purpose, photocopy the 100 square game board (photocopiable page 83) and cut it up to make the individual cards.

HOW TO PLAY
The 100 square provides the playing area for two pencil and paper games involving two players.

100 Squares
The two players take turns to draw numbers out of the bag and colour in the corresponding number on the 100 square in their colour. They do this until all the number squares are coloured in. They then have to identify blocks of their colour where four numbers form a larger square (see Figure 1) and record these on the record sheet.

If a player has more than four of these large blocks, she should pick the four large blocks that have the highest total (adding the four number squares together) and record these. The sixteen numbers are then totalled, and the player with the highest total wins. If a player should get a nine-square block (see Figure 2), she wins outright.

100 Sequences
This game is played as above; but instead of identifying blocks of numbers, players have to look for sequences of three or more consecutive numbers horizontally (e.g. 7, 8, 9) or patterns of 10 in vertical sequences of three or more (e.g. 7, 17, 27). When all the squares have been coloured in, each player picks out the highest sequence of three numbers (either horizontal or vertical), of four numbers and of five numbers. All these are recorded horizontally on the record sheet. They are then totalled and the highest total wins.

So, if a player has 26, 27 and 28 as the highest sequence of three numbers; 4, 14, 24, and 34 as the highest sequence of four numbers; and 8, 9, 10, 11 and 12 as the highest sequence of five numbers, they would be recorded as shown in Figure 3. Note that a sequence can go beyond the end of a game board row, as with 8, 9, 10, 11 and 12 in the example. The record sheet has been devised to enable the children to cross-check the total horizontally and vertically as shown in Figure 3.

GAME VARIATIONS
Without using the record sheet, the children could look for other number patterns in their own colour, such as odd or even number sequences and times table sequences – e.g. 6, 9, 12 would be a sequence of threes.

WHAT YOU NEED
PHOTOCOPIABLE SHEETS
100 square game board sheet 83, number cards sheets 34 and 35, 'How to play' sheet 82, record sheet 84.
FOR CONSTRUCTION
Card, glue, scissors.
FOR PLAYING
Game board, number cards 1 to 100, bag, 2 coloured pencils, 'How to play' sheet, record sheet.

Figure 1

Figure 2

Figure 3

HOW TO PLAY 100 SQUARES OR SEQUENCES

For 2 players.

YOU NEED: 100 square game board, a bag of 1 to 100 number cards, 2 different-coloured pens, record sheet.

❶ Each player chooses a different-coloured pen.

❷ Take it in turns to pick a number card from the bag and fill in the corresponding number on the 100 square using your colour. Do not return the number cards picked to the bag.

❸ Play until all the squares on the board have been coloured.

For Squares: Each player looks for blocks of 4 squares forming a larger square in his own colour. He chooses the four large squares with the highest numbers and records these on the record sheet. The same number cannot be used twice.

46	47
56	57

The numbers are totalled and the player with the highest total wins. However, if a player has a nine-square block of numbers in his colour, he wins outright.

56	57	58
66	67	68
76	77	78

For Sequences: Each player picks out the highest sequence of three numbers, four numbers and five numbers in his own colour and records these on the record sheet.

The numbers are totalled and the player with the highest total wins. You can check your answer by adding the numbers in both directions – vertically and horizontally.

						Totals
3 number sequence	26	27	28			81
4 number sequence	4	14	24	34		76
5 number sequence	8	9	10	11	12	50
Totals	8	13	50	62	74	201

100 SQUARE

1	2	3	4	5	6	7	8	9	10
11	12	13	14	15	16	17	18	19	20
21	22	23	24	25	26	27	28	29	30
31	32	33	34	35	36	37	38	39	40
41	42	43	44	45	46	47	48	49	50
51	52	53	54	55	56	57	58	59	60
61	62	63	64	65	66	67	68	69	70
71	72	73	74	75	76	77	78	79	80
81	82	83	84	85	86	87	88	89	90
91	92	93	94	95	96	97	98	99	100

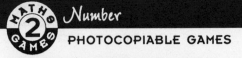

RECORD SHEET FOR 100 SQUARES OR SEQUENCES

SQUARES

9 square beats all

| Name | | Colour |

Pick your best 4 — Total

| Name | | Colour |

Pick your best 4 — Total

SEQUENCES

Pick your best 3
- 3 number sequence
- 4 number sequence
- 5 number sequence

Totals

Name / Colour

Totals — Grand total

Pick your best 3
- 3 number sequence
- 4 number sequence
- 5 number sequence

Totals

Name / Colour

Totals — Grand total

100 TRIANGLE DIAMONDS

TEACHING CONTENT

★ Identifying odd and even numbers (N: 3a; PS: B)
★ Identifying factors of 2, 3, and 5 (N: 3c, PS: E)
★ Developing a range of mental methods for using known facts to find those which they cannot recall (N: 3c; FE: B, C)

PREPARATION

In addition to the game board, 'How to play' and record sheets, you will need a bag of 1 to 100 number cards. These can be made up by photocopying the 100 Square game board (sheet 83) on to card and cutting it up to make individual number cards.

HOW TO PLAY

The 100 Triangle provides the playing area for two pencil and paper games for two players. Each player chooses a different coloured pen. In turn, the players take a card out of the 1 to 100 number bag and colour in that number on the 100 Triangle. Drawn cards are not returned to the bag. Play continues until all the numbers have been coloured in. The players then have to identify 'diamonds' according to the objectives of the particular game being played. The diamonds are pairs of numbers in the same colour and in an upright, not sideways position. Mixed colours do not give diamonds.

Odds and evens diamonds: Each player picks out, in her own colour, either the four highest odd diamonds or the four highest even diamonds. They must be either all odd or all even. These are recorded on the record sheet and the numbers totalled. The player with the highest total wins.

Factors diamonds: Each player picks out, in her own colour, the highest value diamond for each of the factors shown on the record sheet. As there are only two diamonds whose numbers are divisible by both 2 and 3 (30/42 and 36/48) and only one whose numbers are divisible by 5 (25/35), there will be spaces left blank on the record sheet. This imbalance is countered by the bonus number multiplication. The players fill in their diamond numbers on the record sheet and the highest grand total wins.

TEACHER'S ROLE

Ensure that the children understand what it is they are looking for in a diamond. Point out examples: odds (5/11), evens (4/8), factor 2 (12/20), factor 3 (9/15), factors 2 and 3 (30/42), factor 5 (25/35). Before playing, review with the children how to recognise an odd/even number (for Odds and evens), what a factor is and the four different types of number the children will be looking for (Factors). In the interval between playing and recording, go over how to recognise numbers divisible by 2, 3 and 5. *(All even numbers are divisible by 2. Add all digits in a number and divide by 3. If there is no remainder, the number is divisible by 3. Any number ending in 0 or 5 is divisible by 5.)* Draw players' attention to the fact that some numbers can be divisible by more than one of these numbers.

WHAT YOU NEED

PHOTOCOPIABLE SHEETS
100 Triangle Diamonds game board sheet 87, 100 Square game board sheet 83, 'How to play' sheet 86, record sheet 88.

FOR CONSTRUCTION
Card, scissors.

FOR PLAYING
100 Triangle Diamonds game board, bag of 1 to 100 number cards, 'How to play' sheet, record sheet, two different-coloured pens.

Even diamond

Odd diamond

Factor (4) diamond

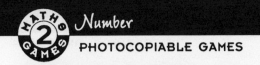

Number
PHOTOCOPIABLE GAMES

SCHOLASTIC PHOTOCOPIABLES
100 TRIANGLE DIAMONDS

HOW TO PLAY 100 TRIANGLE DIAMONDS

For 2 players.

YOU NEED: a 100 Triangle Diamonds game board, a bag of 1 to 100 number cards, a record sheet, 2 different-coloured pens.

❶ Each player chooses a different-coloured pen.

❷ Take it in turns to pick a number card from the bag and fill in the corresponding number on the 100 Triangle using your colour. Do not return the number cards to the bag.

❸ Play until all the numbers on the board have been coloured in. Once this is done, you can play the games below.

ODDS AND EVENS DIAMONDS: Each player looks for vertical diamonds of odd or even numbers in her own colour. She chooses the four highest odd *or* even diamonds (do not mix them!) and records these on the record sheet.

The numbers are totalled and the player with the highest total wins.

FACTORS DIAMONDS: Each player picks out the highest factor 2, factor 3, factors 2 and 3, and factor 5 diamonds in her own colour and records these on the record sheet.

Add the two numbers in each diamond together and then multiply the total by the bonus number on the record sheet. (You can use a calculator!) Add all the subtotals together. The player with the highest grand total wins.

GAME BOARD FOR 100 TRIANGLE DIAMONDS

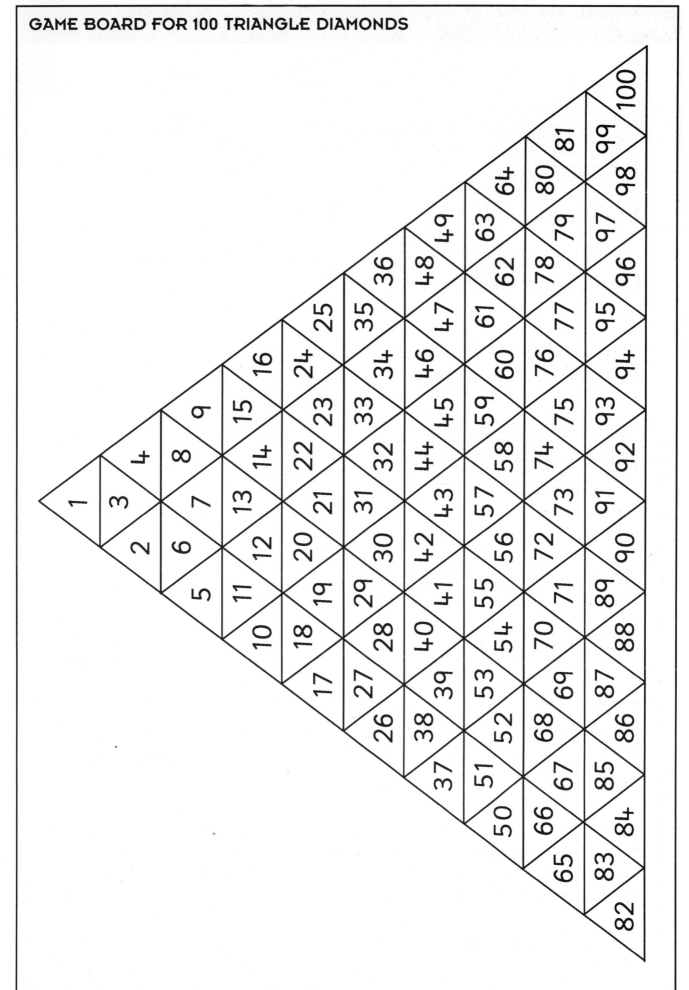

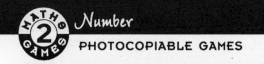

SCHOLASTIC PHOTOCOPIABLES
100 TRIANGLE DIAMONDS

RECORD SHEET FOR 100 TRIANGLE DIAMONDS

ODDS AND EVENS DIAMONDS

Name [ ]

My four highest odd/even diamonds

Add all the numbers together.

Total [ ]

Name [ ]

My four highest odd/even diamonds

Add all the numbers together.

Total [ ]

FACTORS DIAMONDS

Name [ ]

Factor 2   Factors 2 and 3
   Factor 3   Factor 5

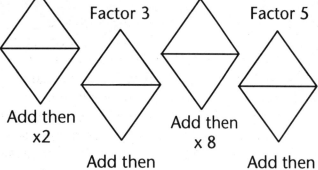

Add then ×2   Add then ×8
   Add then ×5   Add then ×10

⇓   ⇓   ⇓   ⇓
         ⇓   ⇓

[ ] Subtotal   [ ] Subtotal
   [ ] Subtotal   [ ] Subtotal

Grand total [ ]

Name [ ]

Factor 2   Factors 2 and 3
   Factor 3   Factor 5

Add then ×2   Add then ×8
   Add then ×5   Add then ×10

⇓   ⇓   ⇓   ⇓
         ⇓   ⇓

[ ] Subtotal   [ ] Subtotal
   [ ] Subtotal   [ ] Subtotal

Grand total [ ]

Number
PHOTOCOPIABLE GAMES
CARPET TILES

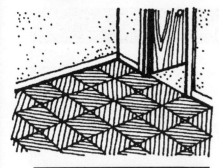

CARPET TILES

TEACHING CONTENT

★ Using coordinates in the first quadrant, recognising the relationship between coordinates of related points on a line or in a shape (N: 3b; SPM: D)

WHAT YOU NEED

PHOTOCOPIABLE SHEETS
Game board sheet 91, carpet tiles sheet 92, 'How to play' sheet 90.
FOR CONSTRUCTION
Card, scissors, coloured crayons.
FOR PLAY
Game board, 'How to play' sheet, a set of carpet tiles for each player, two dice and a shaker.

PREPARATION

Assembling the game: Photocopy the game board (page 91) and carpet tiles (page 92) on to card. Colour in the carpet tiles using crayons if you wish, before cutting up the sheet to make individual tile cards.

Introducing the game: Investigate number grids and simple coordinates with the children before playing this game. Although they may not be aware of it, play with building blocks and square construction tiles can provide a practical representation of coordinates and related points on a line or shape.

HOW TO PLAY

This is a game for two players. Both players use the same game board and their own set of carpet tiles. The players take turns to throw the two dice and use the numbers thrown to make a position on the board. So: if a player throws a 5 and a 2, she can make two possible coordinates on the board (as shown in the illustration). The player chooses one coordinate and places one of her tiles in this position (so that the tile covers the intersection of the two lines). If an opponent's tile is already occupying that position, the tile can be removed and replaced with an opposing tile. The first player to place four tiles together to make a square shape is the winner.

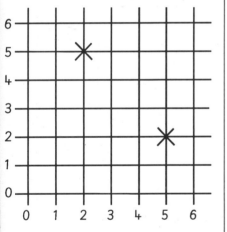

TEACHER'S ROLE

As the game is being played, watch to make sure that the children understand the principles of the game. Are they correctly identifying the positions on the board that they can make from the numbers on the dice? Encourage them to identify both possible positions on the game board, so that they can choose which is the more favourable. It is important that the children place their tiles at the intersections of the two lines and do not try to place the carpet tiles within the adjoining squares. For this reason, the design on both sets of tiles has points at the midway section of each edge – these can be aligned with the gridlines on the game board to make sure the tiles are positioned correctly.

GAME VARIATION

To extend children's understanding of coordinates and quadrants, a game for small groups using two dice and a photocopy of the game board can be played. The teacher throws the two dice and the children take turns to name and circle one of the coordinates that can be made with the two numbers. Are they right? What other coordinate can be made? Draw in rules from these points to the horizontal and vertical axes using different colours, and shade in these areas. What do the children notice about the number of squares within these two shapes? Can they recognise the relationship between the two coordinates and the areas they define?

HOW TO PLAY CARPET TILES

For 2 players.

YOU NEED: a game board, a set of carpet tiles for each player, two dice and a shaker.

❶ Each player collects a set of carpet tiles.

❷ Take turns to throw the two dice. Use the numbers thrown to make two coordinates.

*So: if you throw a 5 and a 2
you can make 5, 2 or 2, 5*

❸ Choose which coordinate you want to use and place one of your tiles in this position on the game board.

Make sure your tile covers the intersection of the two lines on the game board.

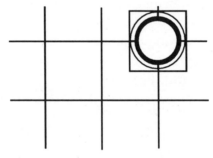

❹ Continue playing. The first player to place four tiles together on the game board to make a square shape is the winner.

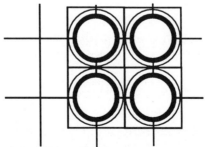

☆REMEMBER!

If you make a coordinate that is already occupied by one of your opponent's tiles, you can remove the tile and replace it with one of your own.

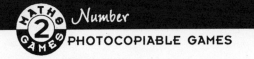

SCHOLASTIC PHOTOCOPIABLES

CARPET TILES

CARPET TILES GAME BOARD

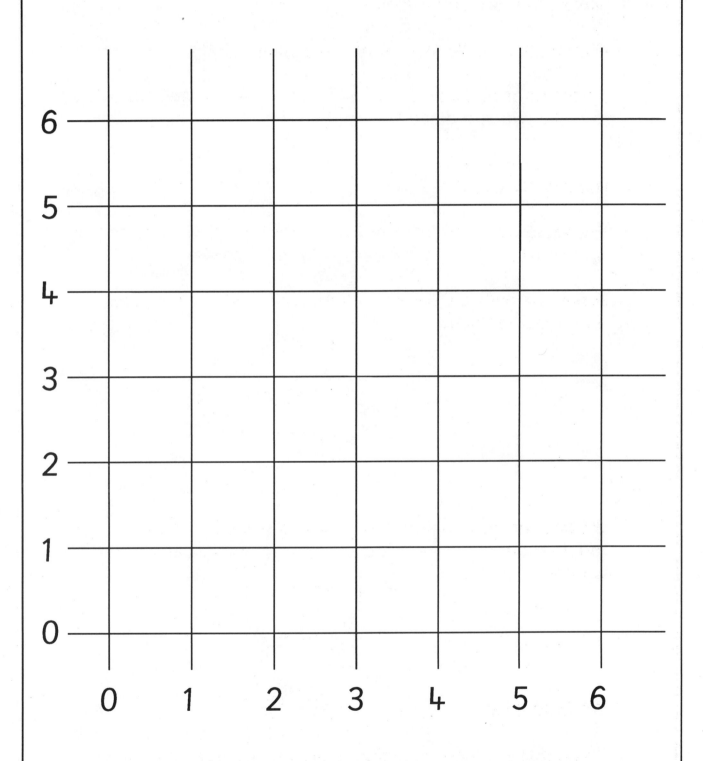

CARPET TILES GAME BOARD

CARPET TILES
Cut up to make two different sets of carpet tiles.

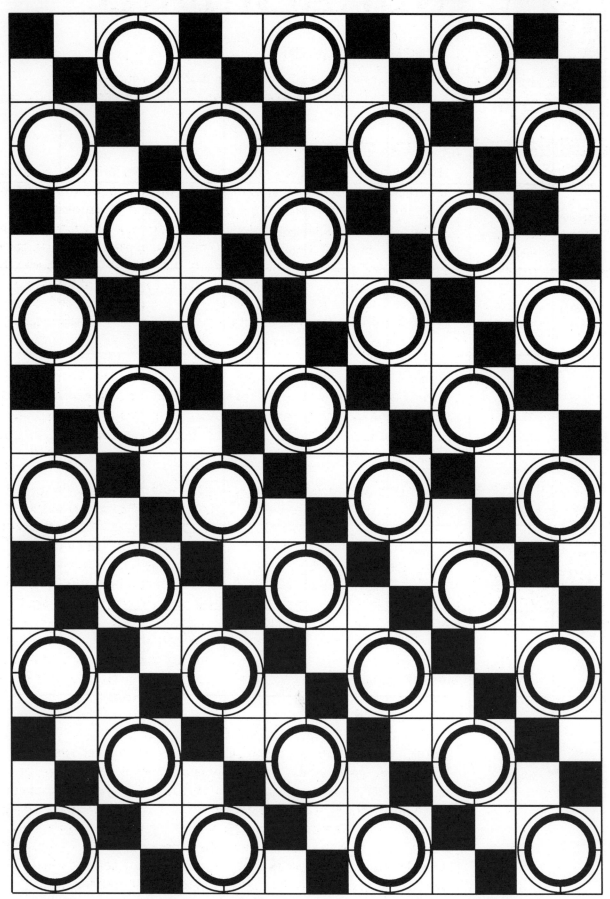

PALACE IN NUMBERLAND

TEACHING CONTENT

★ Using a range of mathematical methods involving addition, subtraction, multiplication and division with numbers to 100 (N: 3c; MD: C)

PREPARATION

Assembling the game: Copy photocopiable sheet 96 four times on to card and stick the sheets together to make the game board, as shown in the diagram below. Fill in each of the starting spaces in the corners of the game board with a different colour (red, blue, green and yellow). The rest of the board can be coloured in with crayons to make it more attractive if you wish. Copy sheet 97 once on to card, then cut out and colour in the palace centre piece before fixing it in place at the centre of the game board. Colour the four playing pieces (each in a colour to match the corner starting squares), then cut them out and construct as indicated. A standard 1 to 6 dice is needed, and a set of single digit number cards (page 34) which will be drawn from a bag.

Introducing the game: Explain that in this game the players must make their way through the Forest of Numberland to the palace, and that the first player to reach the palace wins. Ask the children to make up their own fairy story about why they want to get to the palace.

HOW TO PLAY

This is a game for two to four players. Only one game board is needed. The aim is to move along the track and reach the '10' square at the centre. Each of the players chooses a coloured playing piece and places it on the matching coloured square in the corner of the game board. To start, they must make a score divisible by 2 – the number on the starting square. To do this, they take turns to draw two number cards from the bag and can add, subtract or combine these two numbers to make their score. So if they draw a 2 and a 3, they can make: 5 by adding the two numbers together; 1 by subtracting the 2 from the 3; 6 by multiplying them together; or 23 or 32 by combining the two numbers to make a two-digit number. If a player makes a score that is divisible by 2 then he can throw the dice to determine the number of spaces he can move. If not, he cannot move and must try again next turn. The cards are returned to the bag after each turn. The players then take turns to throw the dice and move their playing pieces along the track, following the direction of the arrows. When a player lands on a number square, he draws two numbers from the bag and tries to make a score divisible by the number on the square. If he is successful, he can throw the dice and move inwards towards the centre; if not, he cannot move and, on his next turn, throws the dice and continues sideways along the track. Only one playing piece can occupy a square at any one time – if a square is already occupied, you cannot move and must wait until the next turn. When a player reaches the '10' square at the centre, he must make a

WHAT YOU NEED

PHOTOCOPIABLE SHEETS
Game board sheet 96, 'How to play' sheet 95, centre piece and playing pieces sheet 97.

FOR CONSTRUCTION
Card, scissors, adhesive, adhesive tape, crayons.

FOR PLAY
A game board, a playing piece for each player, 'How to play' sheet, a bag of single digit number cards, a dice and shaker.

Stick the four tracks together with the centre piece in the middle to make the game board.

score divisible by 10 to win. If he does not make a winning score immediately, he cannot move and tries again next turn. The first player to reach the centre and make a score divisible by 10 is the winner.

TEACHER'S ROLE

This game requires flexibility of thought, in that the players must decide on the best way to use the numbers available to make a favourable score. Encourage the children to consider all of the possibilities in order to extend their number manipulation skills. What are the different scores you can make using these two numbers? Can any of them be divided by the number on the square? This will help them to develop a greater awareness of multiplication and division facts – that numbers divisible by 2 end in 0, 2, 4, 6 or 8, numbers divisible by 5 end in 5 and 0, and so on. It may be advisable for the children to use a calculator to check that their score is actually divisible by the number on the square, to avoid any mistakes.

GAME VARIATION

The range of number cards in the bag can be restricted by the teacher to match the ability of the children if necessary.

HOW TO PLAY PALACE IN NUMBERLAND

For 2 to 4 players.

YOU NEED: a game board, a playing piece for each player, a dice, a bag of single digit number cards, a calculator.

❶ Each player chooses a playing piece and places it on the corner starting square of the board in the matching colour (the blue playing piece on the blue square, and so on). Each starting square is marked with the number 2.

❷ Take turns to draw two number cards from the bag. You must try to make a number that can be divided by 2 using these two numbers. You can add, subtract or multiply the numbers, or combine them to make a two-digit number.

So: If you draw a 3 and a 2, you can make: 3 + 2 = 5 or 3 − 2 = 1 or 3 x 2 = 6, or the numbers can be combined to make 32 or 23.

If you can make a number that divides by 2, throw the dice and move that number of spaces, in the direction of the arrows.

❸ Continue to take turns throwing the dice. A player landing on a number square, draws two number cards from the bag and tries to make a number that divides by the number on the square.

If he succeeds, he throws the dice again and moves in towards the centre. If not, he cannot move and must continue sideways round the board on his next turn.

❹ The first player to reach the palace and draw two cards to make a number divisible by 10 is the winner.

☆ REMEMBER!

The palace square is the only square that can hold more than one playing piece at a time. If any other square to which you want to move is occupied, that turn does not count.

Number
PHOTOCOPIABLE GAMES
PALACE IN NUMBERLAND

CENTRE PIECE
See page 93 for construction diagram.

PLAYING PIECES
Cut out, fold, stick and hold.

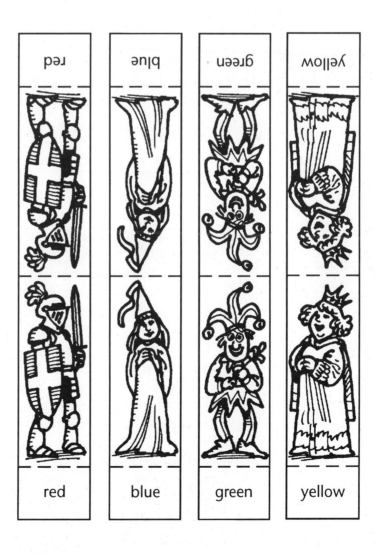

97

PHOTOCOPIABLE GAMES — MT. PROBABILITY

MT. PROBABILITY

TEACHING CONTENT

★ Handling data (HD: 1b, 2a, b, c; IH: B, C)
★ Developing an understanding of probability (HD: 3a, c)

PREPARATION

In this teacher-directed game, each child in the group plays individually, and rejoins the others at the end to discuss and compare results. As such, it requires a span of time that allows each individual to complete her record sheet. The whole class can play, with each child having her 'go' in spare moments. Two dice are needed, one white 1 to 6 dice and one coloured 1 to 6 dice. Before the children begin to play, make sure they understand the general aim, what they have to do and how the record sheet works – in particular, that they understand how to enter the tallies.

HOW TO PLAY

Each player has to climb up and down the mountain, creating and recording data about her climb as she goes. The right combinations of the two dice must be thrown at each stage, going in order from 2 to 12. To start, a 1 and 1 have to be thrown. For the next stage either of two combinations, 2 and 1 or 1 and 2, can be thrown. And so on. The player must achieve each step before moving on to the next. A record of how many throws it takes to achieve this is made using grouped tally marks and then totalling these. So, if a player takes 41 throws to get 1 and 1, she will have recorded the tallies and total as shown (see left). Each player continues until she reaches 12.

TEACHER'S ROLE

When everyone has completed a sheet, bring the class together to collate the data and discover who climbed the mountain fastest at each stage and overall (the number of throws representing time). Ask each child how many throws it took to get 1 and 1. Keep a running total on the chalkboard. Everyone enters the final total on their record sheet. Go through this for each stage. Ask the children to use these new data to work out the average number of throws for each step up and down the mountain, and the average total number of throws for the whole climb. Make sure they understand how to work this out.

When everyone has completed this, bring the class together again and discuss their results. What conclusions can they draw about probability at each step of the climb? Do they see that the range of possible number combinations at each step is significant? Clearly, it is easier the higher up the mountain you go; at the summit (7), there are six possible combinations, so achieving this step should take far less time than the first or last step. Can they work out the number of combinations and the odds for a particular number? The record sheet indicates that there is a total of 36 possible combinations. So, to achieve 2 (1 and 1), there is 1 chance in 36; to achieve 3, there are 2 in 36 (or 1 in 18); and so on.

Find out who was the fastest at each stage (11 possible winners) and who was the fastest overall (players will need to add up their total number of throws for all stages).

WHAT YOU NEED

PHOTOCOPIABLE SHEETS
Record sheet 99.
FOR PLAYING
A record sheet and pencil for each player, one white 1 to 6 dice, one coloured 1 to 6 dice, a shaker.

	2
Tally marks	｜｜｜｜ ｜｜｜｜ ｜｜｜｜ ｜｜｜｜ ｜｜｜｜ ｜｜｜｜ ｜｜｜｜ ｜｜｜｜ ｜

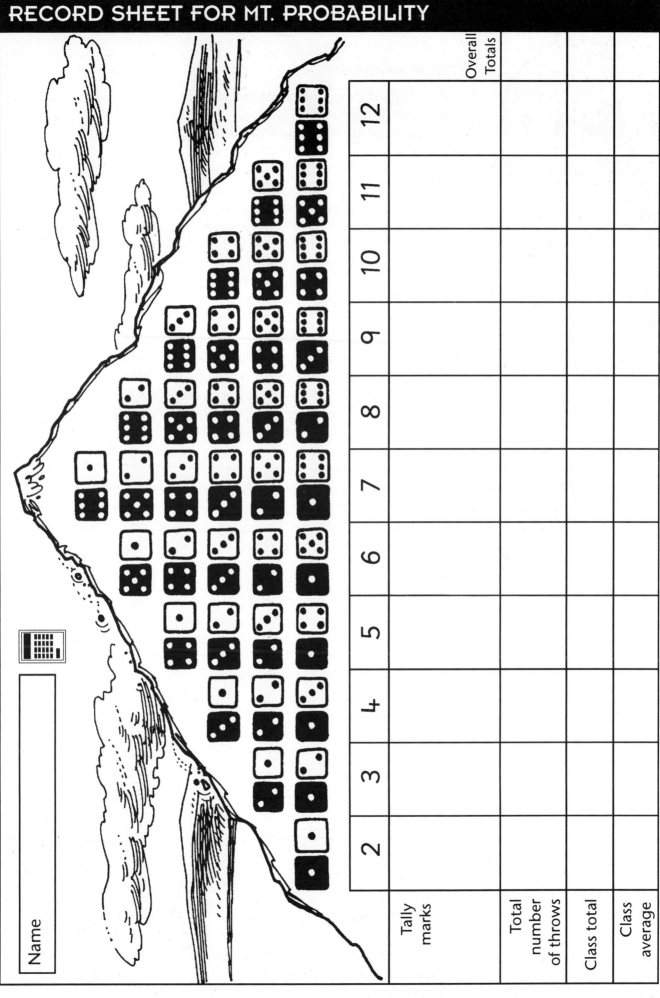

GRAND PRIX

TEACHING CONTENT

★ Creating and interpreting frequency tables showing grouped discrete data (N: 3a; IH: C)
★ Practising addition with numbers 1 to 12 (N: 3c; RTN: A)

PREPARATION

Assembling the game: Photocopy the track on sheet 103 four times and sheet 104 once on to card, and assemble the game board as shown below with the centre piece in the middle. Colour in the racing car playing pieces, then cut them out, fold and stick together. Colour in each of the 'lap recorder' lines on the game board in colours to match the cars and draw in a starting grid on one of the track squares. The penalty cards and the rest of the game board can be coloured in to make the game more attractive.

Introducing the game: Motor racing is a high-profile sport. Ask the children what they can tell you about it. Do they understand that the cars travel round and round the same track and that each circuit is called a 'lap'? Do they know that the first driver to complete a set number of laps is the winner? Discuss motor racing vocabulary – pit stop, starting grid, steward and so on – to help the children understand the sport.

HOW TO PLAY

This is a game for four players. Each of the players chooses a coloured playing piece and a counter in the matching colour. All of the playing pieces are placed on the starting grid of the track and the counter is placed on the '1' of the lap recorder in the same colour. Place all of the penalty/bonus cards in the space at the centre of the game board. The players take turns to throw the two dice and move their playing pieces around the track according to the total number thrown. If a player lands on the entrance to a pit stop, he can only leave by throwing a double (then throwing again, in his next turn, to move on). If a player lands on a 'card' square, he must take the top card from the centre pile and follow

WHAT YOU NEED

PHOTOCOPIABLE SHEETS
Race track sheet 103, playing pieces sheet 104, penalty cards sheets 105 and 106, 'How to play' sheet 102, record sheet 107.

FOR CONSTRUCTION
Card, scissors, adhesive, coloured crayons.

FOR PLAYING
Game board, 'How to play' sheet, playing pieces, four counters (red, blue, green, yellow), a record sheet, a dice and shaker.

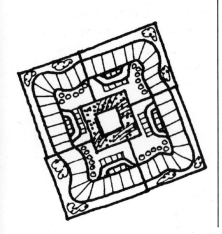

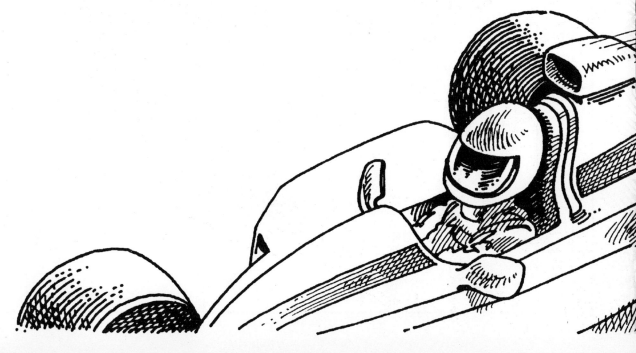

the instruction. The card is returned to the bottom of the pile and play continues. When moving backwards, players should not go past the start line. Each time a player throws the dice, he records a tally mark in the appropriate 'lap' box on the record sheet; and each time a lap is completed, he moves his counter on one space to show which lap he is on. If the 'race stops now' card is drawn, then the player who is in the lead wins. If the race is stopped on the first or second lap, then it is restarted. If the race lasts to the sixth lap, then the first player to complete the last lap is the winner and the other players complete the lap they are on, then work out their finishing positions.

TEACHER'S ROLE

During the game, watch to make sure that the children are following the rules correctly. Do they understand that the lap recorder indicates the number of laps completed? Can they see how important it is that they use this correctly? Make sure that each throw is recorded by a tally mark in the correct box on the record sheet. At the end of the game, the players can count up the number of throws they took to complete each lap and then work out which car was the fastest on each lap. Can they see that the car that took the least number of throws was the fastest? What is the lap record? Ask the children to calculate their average number of throws per lap. Compare their averages with their finishing positions. Do they notice any relationship? What difference would it make if they had not recorded their turns for each lap accurately? Would their finishing positions match the order of their average scores? If not, could they see where they had gone wrong? If a player is disqualified, he can work out the average for the number of laps he has completed. The same applies for all of the players if the race is stopped.

HOW TO PLAY GRAND PRIX

For 4 players.

YOU NEED: the game board, a playing piece and counter for each player, the record sheet, a pencil, two dice and a shaker, a pencil.

❶ Each player chooses a racing car and the counter in the matching colour. Place all of the racing cars on the starting grid of the track, and the counters on the '1' space of the lap recorder grid in the same colour (the red counter on the red lap recorder grid, and so on).

❷ Take turns to throw the dice and move the cars along the track according to the total number thrown. Each time you throw the dice, put a tally mark in the box next to that lap number on the record sheet.

❸ If you land on the entrance to a pit stop, you must throw a double to leave. When you throw a double, move out to the small arrow.

❹ If you land on a 'card' square, you must pick the top card from the pile at the centre of the game board. Follow the instruction on the card, then return it to the bottom of the pile.

So: if you draw the 'Skid on oil (–5)' card you must move back 5 squares.

If moving backwards, you must NOT go past the start line.

❺ Each time you complete a lap, you can move your counter on the lap recorder to show which lap you are on.

❻ The first player to complete six laps is the winner. The other players complete the lap they are on to find their finishing positions.

☆ REMEMBER!

If the 'Race stops now' card is drawn, stop playing and the player in the lead is the winner. BUT if the race is stopped before two laps have been completed then the race must be restarted.

If you have to go into the pits, you must throw a double before you can move on.

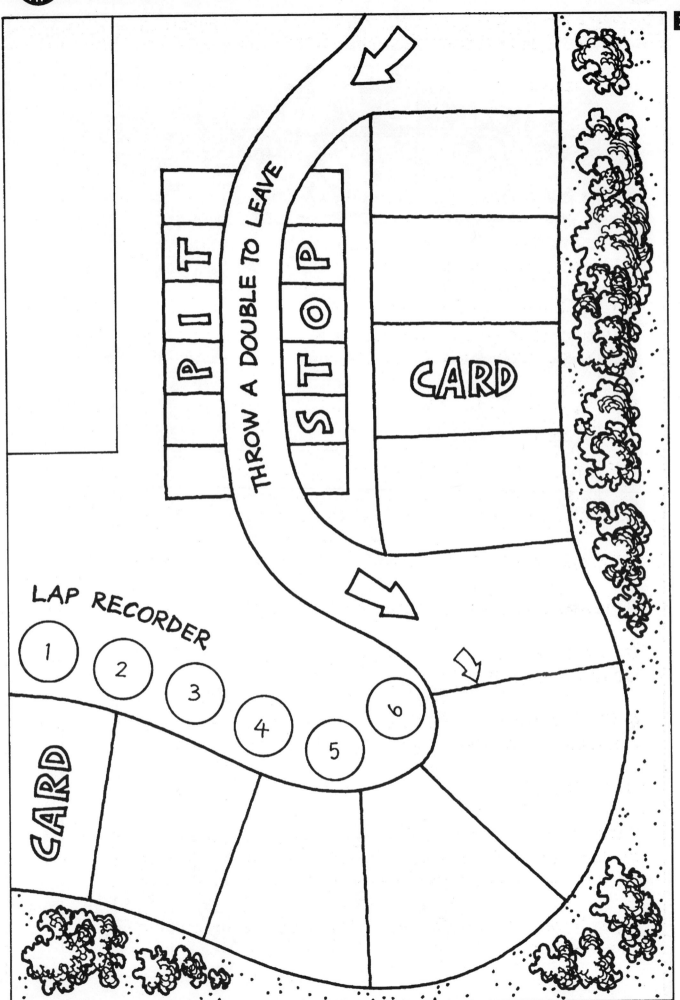

Number
PHOTOCOPIABLE GAMES

SCHOLASTIC PHOTOCOPIABLES

GRAND PRIX

CENTRE PIECE   See page 100 for construction diagram.

cards

PLAYING PIECES

Colour one playing piece in each of the following colours: red, blue, green and yellow. Cut out, fold, stick and hold.

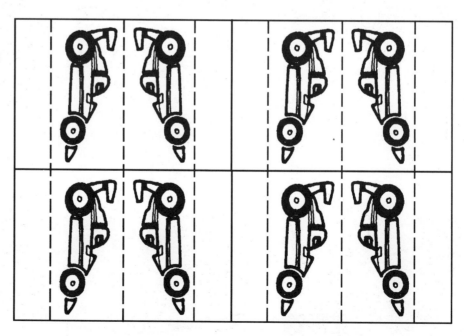

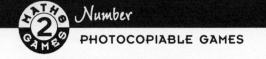

PENALTY CARDS
Cut up this sheet to make individual cards.

Crash: race stops now. 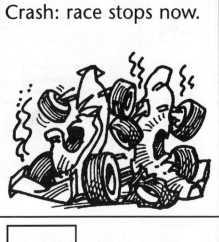	**-4** Spin. 	**+3** Accelerating well. 
-4 Gears stick. 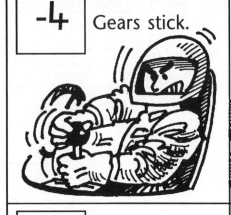	**+5** Easy overtake. 	**-6** Puncture. 
-7 Rain. 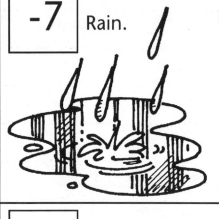	**-2** Fuel low. 	**-5** Skid on oil. 
+3 New tyres. 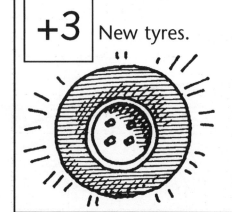	**-1** Steward on track. 	**-10** Overtaking dangerously. 

RECORD SHEET FOR GRAND PRIX

Tick for each throw.

red	driver		
lap 1		lap 4	
lap 2		lap 5	
lap 3		lap 6	
blue	driver		
lap 1		lap 4	
lap 2		lap 5	
lap 3		lap 6	
green	driver		
lap 1		lap 4	
lap 2		lap 5	
lap 3		lap 6	
yellow	driver		
lap 1		lap 4	
lap 2		lap 5	
lap 3		lap 6	

race summary

lap 1	fastest car	colour	number of throws	
lap 2	fastest car	colour	number of throws	
lap 3	fastest car	colour	number of throws	
lap 4	fastest car	colour	number of throws	
lap 5	fastest car	colour	number of throws	
lap 6	fastest car	colour	number of throws	

1st	colour	2nd	colour	3rd	colour	4th	colour

SUPER SAVER DAY

TEACHING CONTENT

★ Calculating percentages with numbers to two decimal places in the context of money (N: 2b; RTN: D)
★ Using the functions of a basic calculator to work out mathematical problems (N: 4a; RTN: C)

PREPARATION

Assembling the game: Photocopy pages 40, 41 and 42 on to card and assemble the supermarket game board as indicated on page 37. The shelves of the supermarket can be coloured in before assembly to make the game board more attractive. If you wish, a 'wall' can be included as an extension of the baseboard so that the supermarket has entrance and exit doors. Colour in the shopping trolley playing pieces, then cut them out, fold them and stick them together. Cut out the percentage spinner on page 110 and push a matchstick through the centre. The record sheet on page 111 can be photocopied on to paper, as it can only be used once.

Introducing the game: Most children will have visited a supermarket and be familiar with how they are laid out and how shoppers walk up and down the aisles in order to purchase the items that they require. It is likely that they will also have seen signs advertising percentage discounts on certain products, and they may have some idea of what this means. This activity will help them to understand and calculate percentage discounts. The children will need experience of writing decimal prices and calculating percentages to play this game.

WHAT YOU NEED

PHOTOCOPIABLE PAGES
Supermarket baseboard sheet 40, supermarket aisle sheets 41 and 42, shopping trolley playing pieces sheet 39, 'How to play' sheet 110, record sheet 111.

FOR CONSTRUCTION
Card, scissors, adhesive, coloured crayons, a matchstick.

FOR PLAYING
Supermarket game board, 'How to play' sheet, a percentage spinner, a shopping trolley playing piece for each player, a record sheet and pencil for each player, a dice and shaker, a calculator.

SUPER SAVER DAY

HOW TO PLAY

This is a game for two to four players. Each player needs a trolley playing piece, a pencil and a record sheet. The players take turns to roll the dice and, starting from the entrance to the supermarket, move their trolleys along the track according to the number thrown. Each time a player lands on a square he must buy that item, but he also receives a percentage discount determined by a throw of the spinner: 10%, 20%, 25% or 33%. The percentage, name and price of the item and the amount of money saved are then recorded on the record sheet. Play continues until all of the players have completed the journey along the supermarket track; then they all add up the total value of the savings they have made. The player with the highest total savings is the winner.

TEACHER'S ROLE

As the game is in progress, check that the children are calculating the percentages correctly and point them in the right direction if necessary. It is important that they understand how the percentage calculations work, and develop a concept of roughly what the answer should be. For this reason, it is important that all prices are entered as decimal figures. Ask questions to develop this mental checking process, so that if the answer is much too large or much too small in relation to the original price, the children will recognise that they have probably made an error in their calculation and try again. Encourage the children to calculate the percentages on a calculator without using the '%' function, so that the calculator is only used as a tool and they do the mathematical thinking themselves. It is important that the answers to their calculations should be a realistic representation of money values (to two decimal places), so it may be necessary to round their figures up. Children may need some help with this process. This game also provides a good opportunity for discussion and role-play, and can be used to introduce the children to the vocabulary involved in the mathematical side of shopping: recommended price, percentage discount, retail price and so on. If the children see that the maths they are doing has a significance in the real world, it will make their work more meaningful.

HOW TO PLAY SUPER SAVER DAY

For 2 to 4 players.

YOU NEED: a supermarket game board, a trolley playing piece and record sheet for each player, pencils, a percentage spinner, a dice and shaker, a calculator.

❶ Each player chooses a shopping trolley playing piece and places it at the entrance of the supermarket.

❷ Take it in turns to throw the dice and move along the track.

❸ Each time your trolley lands on a square you must buy that item, BUT the item is to be bought at a percentage discount. In order to find out the discount, spin the percentage spinner. You can then work out the amount of money you have saved using a calculator.

So: if you land on the 'eggs' square (£1.10) and the spinner lands on 33%, 1.10 x 33 ÷ 100 = 0.363
Round up the answer to the nearest penny (in this case £0.36)
This is the amount of money you have saved!

❹ Write down the name, price and amount of money you have saved for each item you buy on the record sheet. Make sure you have worked out the discount correctly and written it down properly.

❺ Play until all players have been round the board.

❻ Now add up the total amount of money you have saved. The player with the highest total is the winner.

PERCENTAGE SPINNER
Cut out the spinner and mount on to card. Push a matchstick through its centre.

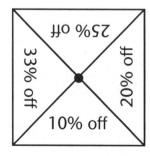

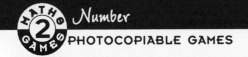

SCHOLASTIC PHOTOCOPIABLES
SUPER SAVER DAY

RECORD SHEET FOR SUPER SAVER DAY

%	Item/price	Money saved	%	Item/price	Money saved
		●		subtotal	●
		●			●
		●			●
		●			●
		●			●
		●			●
		●			●
		●			●
		●			●
		●			●
		●			●
		●			●
		●			●
		●			●
		●			●
		●			●
		●			●
		●			●
	subtotal	●		total discount	●

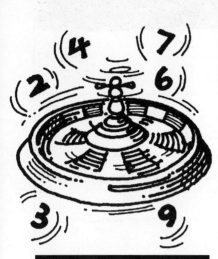

NUMBER ROULETTE

TEACHING CONTENT

★ Reading, writing and ordering whole numbers up to 10 000 to develop understanding of place value (N: 2a; RTN: C)
★ Using a calculator to check results and find solutions to problems (N: 1b, 3g, 4c; IH: C)
★ Introducing the concept of average (HD: 2c; IH: E)

PREPARATION

You will need to construct the Number meter from the Special section (page 144). Explain to the children how the meter works. It's rather like an old-fashioned gas meter and can demonstrate numbers from 0000 to 9999. The basic activity of creating and recording the numbers can be set up in a corner of the room, and players can 'have their go' individually at odd moments during the day. Put out the Number meter, the record sheet (page 113), the dice and shaker and some pencils.

HOW TO PLAY

This is a teacher-directed, large-group game in which individual players create a 4-digit number. The numbers are then averaged and the player whose number is closest to the average wins.

Each player has three throws of the dice for each wheel of the meter. In turn, starting with the units wheel, the wheels are moved according to the dice throws. So if the first throw is 6, the second is 5 and the third is 2, the units wheel would finally end up at 3. (In this game there is no adding on from wheel to wheel.) The same is done for the tens, hundreds and thousands wheels. When the 4-digit number has been created, it is written in with the player's name on the record sheet. When all the players have recorded their numbers, the group comes together to work out and discuss the final results under the teacher's direction.

TEACHER'S ROLE

Besides setting the game up and explaining the procedure, the teacher should bring the group together at the end to explain how to work out the average and the final positions. Emphasise the words 'average' and 'spread'. The **average** is the total of the 4-digit numbers divided by however many players' numbers there are. The **spread** is the range of players' 4-digit numbers, from the lowest to the highest.

EXTENSION

★ Practising subtraction with four-digit numbers using a calculator (N: 3d, g, h, 4a, c; AS: D)

Use the alternative record sheet on page 114. Each player creates two numbers and then finds the difference using a calculator. At the end, the differences are averaged and the player with the difference closest to the average difference is the winner.

WHAT YOU NEED

PHOTOCOPIABLE SHEETS
Number meter sheet 144, record sheet 113 (or record sheet 114 for extension).

FOR CONSTRUCTION
Card, glue, scissors, 4 paper fasteners or card rivets.

FOR PLAYING
Number meter, record sheet (or record sheet for extension), dice and shaker, calculator, pencils.

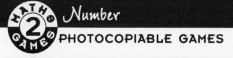

RECORD SHEET FOR NUMBER ROULETTE

Name	Number	Position

Everyone makes a 4-digit number, using the dice and the Number meter.

| + | all numbers = ☐ total

| ÷ | by number of players. Average is ☐

The nearest number to the average wins. Work out the final positions.

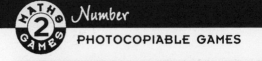

RECORD SHEET FOR NUMBER ROULETTE (EXTENSION)

Name	1st number	2nd number	Difference	Position

Everyone makes two 4-digit numbers, using the dice and the Number meter. To find the average difference:

☐ + all differences = ☐ total

☐ ÷ by number of players. Average difference is ☐

The nearest difference to the average wins. Work out the final positions.

114

CHOC SHOP

WHAT YOU NEED

PHOTOCOPIABLE SHEETS
'How to play' sheet 116, record sheet 117.

FOR PLAYING
'How to play' sheet, record sheet, one white 1 to 6 dice, one coloured 1 to 6 dice, a shaker, a different-coloured pen for each player, a calculator.

TEACHING CONTENT

☆ Solving problems using fractions in context (N: 2c, 4a; FPR: C)
☆ Expressing fractions in equivalent forms and decimals (N: 2b; RTN: D)
☆ Finding simple fractions of quantities and computing their differences using a calculator (N: 3g; FPR: C)

PREPARATION

One record sheet is shared by all players. Additionally, two 1 to 6 dice are required: one white, the other in a different colour. The children should be familiar with the terms **numerator** (top number of a fraction) and **denominator** (bottom number of a fraction). Review the fact that fractions are parts of a whole number and that 1 = 2/2, 3/3, 4/4 and so on. Explain that the chocolate shop has lots of chocolate bars that are the same size, but they are divided into different numbers of sections from 2 to 12. Each player is going to have a chance to win part of a bar, but who will get the biggest piece?

HOW TO PLAY

The aim of this game for two to four players is to get the biggest piece of chocolate. Each player in turn throws the white dice first. This gives his numerator, and is recorded on the record sheet. The white dice is left there, and the coloured dice is then thrown. The throw of this dice and the throw of the first dice, added together, form the denominator. So, if the first dice throw is 3 and the second is 4, the resulting fraction is 3/7. The player finds the chocolate bar with the same number of sections as his denominator and colours in the number of sections indicated by his numerator. Once a chocolate bar has been coloured in, no other player can use it. Each player must throw the dice until a new denominator is reached. When everyone has had a go, the players use a calculator to divide numerator by denominator, to find out who won the biggest mouthful. The player who gets nearest to 1 is the winner.

TEACHER'S ROLE

The game requires that the children make a three-way connection with fractions. First they have to create a vulgar fraction, identifying the numerator and denominator. Be on hand to explain or review these terms. Children will remember them far more readily if they are using them in a realistic context at the time. Then the children have to pick out which bar of chocolate is already divided into the same number of parts as the denominator and colour in the number of parts demanded by the numerator. This requires visualising the fraction in terms of something real. Finally, the children need to compare the different fractions to find out who won the biggest 'bite'. It is not always easy to *see* which is the biggest, for instance to compare three-eighths and five-elevenths; this is reinforced in the illustration on the record sheet. One way is to find a common denominator and multiply. However, for this game, children are required to divide the numerator by the denominator (using a calculator) to see that the bigger the fraction, the nearer it is to 1. After the game, discuss equivalent fractions with the children.

HOW TO PLAY CHOC SHOP

For 2 to 4 players.

YOU NEED: a record sheet, one white 1 to 6 dice, one coloured 1 to 6 dice, a shaker, a different-coloured pen for each player, a calculator.

❶ Decide your playing order and write your names on the record sheet.

❷ Each player in turn throws the white dice first. This gives the numerator for your fraction. Write this in on the record sheet.

❸ Leave the white dice where it is and throw the coloured dice. Add the throw of the coloured dice and the throw of the white dice together to get your denominator.

So: if your first dice throw is 3 and the second is 4, the resulting fraction is:

$$\boxed{3} + \boxed{4} = \frac{3}{7}$$

❹ Find the chocolate bar with the same number of sections as your denominator, and colour in the number of sections indicated by your numerator.

❺ When everyone has had a go, use a calculator to divide numerator by denominator, to find out who won the biggest mouthful. The player who gets nearest to 1 is the winner.

☆ REMEMBER!

Once a chocolate bar has been coloured in, no other player can use it. Each player must throw until a new denominator is reached.

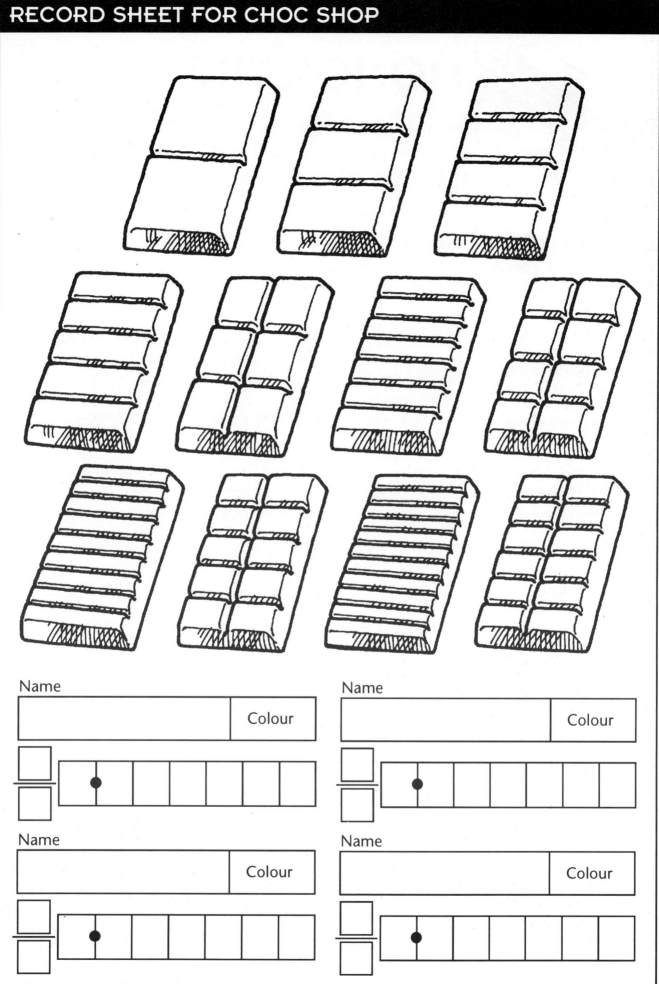

NUMBER MONORAIL

TEACHING CONTENT

★ Understanding the relationship between positive and negative numbers (N: 2b; RTN: E)
★ Using a plus and minus number line as an introduction to the base coordinate of the four quadrants (N: 3b; RTN: E)

PREPARATION

Assembling the game: Photocopy pages 121 and 122 on to card. Cut out the monorail strips, then fold and stick them end to end to make the monorail as indicated below. Make the monotrain playing piece as indicated on page 122, and ensure that it moves freely along the track. A dice restricted to the values 1 to 3 is needed – this can be made by covering 4, 5 and 6 on a standard dice and drawing in the values 1 to 3 with matching values on opposite faces. A coin showing the signs '+' and '–' is also needed – this can be made by sticking labels on to each face of the coin and using a pen to label one side '+' and the other '–'.

WHAT YOU NEED

PHOTOCOPIABLE SHEETS
Monorail track sheets 121 and 122, monorail train sheet 122, 'How to play' sheet 120.

FOR CONSTRUCTION
Scissors, adhesive, a coin, a dice, sticky labels, a pen.

FOR PLAYING
Monorail track and train, a 1 to 3 dice, a '+' and '–' coin.

The window of the monorail train indicates its position on the track. In the above example the train is at '–3'.

Introducing the game: Even if they have not seen monorails, children will be familiar with railways and how trains travel along tracks to destinations at various points along the line. Discuss how minus numbers are to the left of 0 and plus numbers to the right. Although this is essentially an addition and subtraction game, children need some understanding of positive and negative numbers to play it with confidence.

NUMBER MONORAIL

HOW TO PLAY

This is a game for two or more players. All of the players use the same monorail and train playing piece. The players take turns to throw the restricted dice to find the number of spaces they can move along the track and then spin the coin to find out the direction in which they should move. For example: if a player throws a 3 and a '–' she moves 3 spaces backwards (to the left). Play continues with the players moving the train backwards and forwards along the track. The first player to move the train back to the 0 point on the track is the winner, but the train must land on the 0 point at the end of their move – if their score takes the train past the 0 point in either direction, then play continues. If a player's score takes the train beyond Plus City or Minus Town (the ends of the monorail), then that turn does not count and play passes to the next player.

TEACHER'S ROLE

Observe the players during the game to make sure they understand how the moves are calculated. It is important that they add/subtract their score from the position of the train on the track, and do not see their score as a point on the track to which they should move. A score of '–3' means that they should move 3 spaces backwards, not move to the –3 position on the number line. Make the distinction between their score as part of a calculation and the numbered positions on the number line, to provide the basis for work on coordinates. The children could record the moves of the train to give a numerical representation of their scores for future reference, and can then see who completed the game in the least number of turns. For example:

$0 - 3 = -3 \qquad -3 + 1 = -2 \qquad -2 - 2 = -4 \qquad$ and so on.

The record of 'moves' can be used to recreate the sequence of moves, providing a sort of action replay.

GAME VARIATIONS

★ The objective of the game could be for the train to reach either Plus City or Minus Town, rather than Central Station; but as before, only by scoring the exact number of spaces to take the train to its destination can a player win.

★ The length of the track (and the range of the number points) can be extended according to the ability of the children. In this case, it may be best if an unrestricted 1 to 6 dice is used.

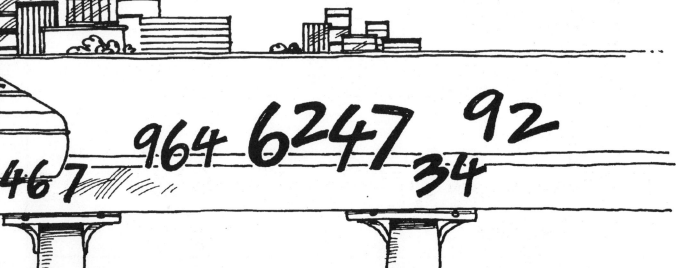

HOW TO PLAY NUMBER MONORAIL

For 2 or more players.

YOU NEED: the monorail and train playing piece, a restricted 1 to 3 dice, a '+' and '−' coin.

❶ Place the train on the monorail track so that the open window shows the 0. The window is used to mark the position of the train on the track during the game.

❷ Take turns to roll the dice, then spin the coin. The dice tells you the number of spaces you can move the train and the coin tells you in which direction the train must be moved.

*So: if you score a 3 and a '+'
the train moves 3 spaces to the right (you add the score on).
But: if you roll a 3 and a '−'
the train moves 3 spaces to the left (you subtract the score).*

❸ Continue playing, moving the train each turn. The player whose score brings the train back to the Central Station at 0 is the winner.

☆ REMEMBER!

The train must stop on 0 for a player to win. If a score takes the train to a point past 0 in either direction, then play continues.

If a score takes the train beyond Plus City or Minus Town (the points at each end of the track), then that turn does not count and play passes to the next player.

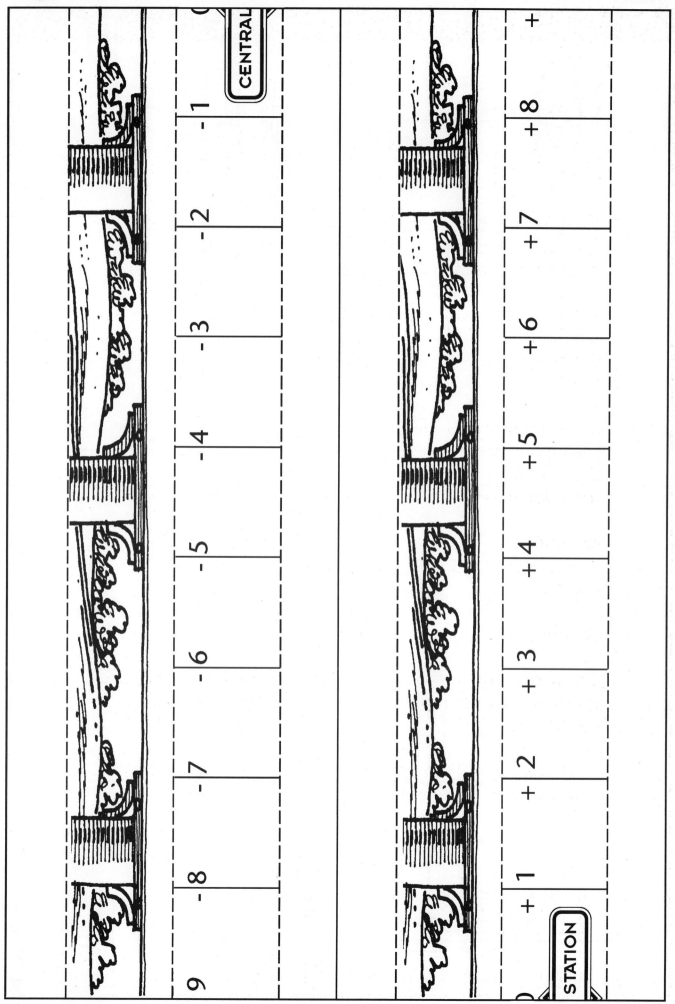

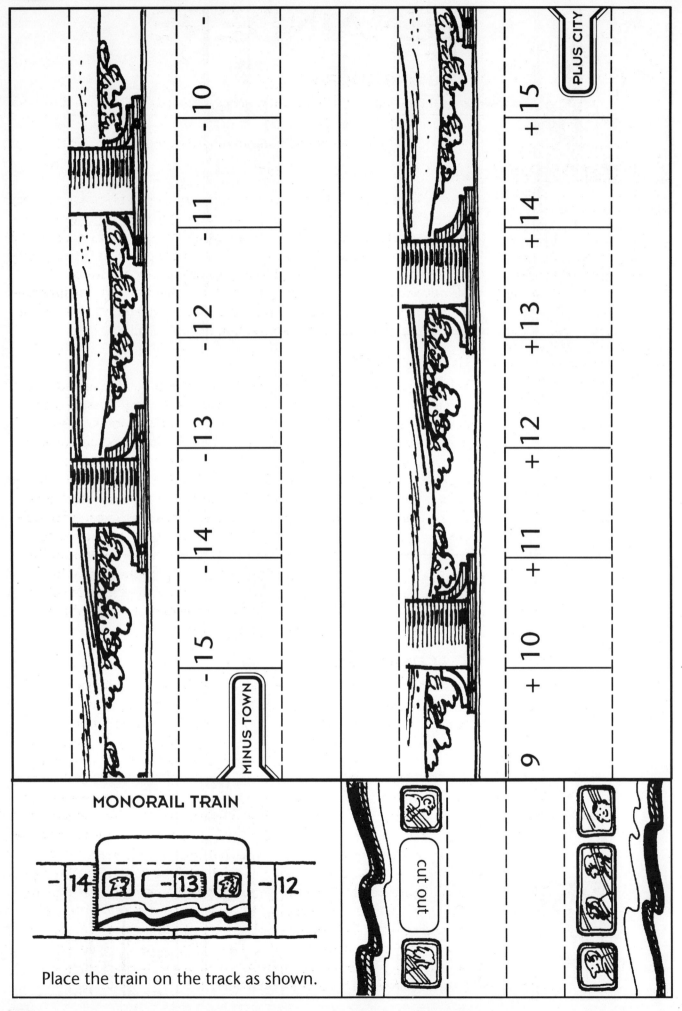

REMAINDERS

WHAT YOU NEED

PHOTOCOPIABLE SHEETS
Single digit number cards sheet 34, double digit number cards sheet 35, record sheet 125, 'How to play' sheet 124.

FOR CONSTRUCTION
Scissors, card, paper, a bag.

FOR PLAYING
'How to play' sheet, a record strip for each player, a bag of single digit number cards, a bag of double digit number cards, pencil, a calculator.

TEACHING CONTENT

★ Understanding the relationship between the four operations, including inverses (N: 3f; AS: D; MD: D)
★ Choose calculation methods appropriate to a problem (N: 3d)

PREPARATION

Assembling the game: Photocopy the single digit and double digit number cards sheets 34 and 35 on to card, then cut up the sheets to make individual cards. Place each set into a separate bag. It is more economical to photocopy the record strips on sheet 125 on to paper, as they can only be used once. Cut up this sheet to make individual record strips.

Introducing the game: Children will need to be familiar with the processes of long multiplication and division to play this game and understand the concepts of remainder and decimal numbers.

HOW TO PLAY

This is a game for two or more players. Each player needs a record strip and a pencil. The first player draws a card from the bag of single digit numbers and another from the bag of double digit numbers. These numbers are then used to make as big a three-digit number as possible, which is then entered in the first box on the record sheet. Thus if he draws a 5 and a 27, he can make either 527 or 275; so 527 is chosen. The chosen number is entered on the record strip. The cards are returned to the bag, and the player then draws another card from the bag of double digit numbers to give the number for the second entry on the record strip. The other players then take turns to draw number cards from the bags to give them their two starting numbers. All of the players then complete the calculation process on their record strip using a calculator. The player with the highest remainder is the winner. The rest of the players work out their positions in descending order.

TEACHER'S ROLE

This activity involves all four number operations and highlights the remainder element of division calculations. Prior to the game, demonstrate the inability of a calculator to give a whole number 'remainder'. Ask the children to work out 105 divided by 11 without using a calculator. Is there a remainder? Then use a calculator to do the division. In the first instance the remainder is 6, but with the calculator the answer is 9.5454545. Are there circumstances when one method of division is better than another? If we are dealing with pure numbers, or if it is possible to break down the objects involved into fractions of a whole, then the decimal answer can be used; but what if the objects cannot be broken down? For example, if a class of 23 children has to be seated at tables in groups of 4, how many tables would be needed? In real terms, there will be 5 tables of 4 and 3 children left over. On a calculator, 23 divided by 4 is 5.75. Can the children see that they need to choose the most appropriate method of calculation? If the game is played with a large group, record sheets can be mounted in a column going down from the largest remainder to the smallest.

HOW TO PLAY REMAINDERS

For 2 or more players.

YOU NEED: a pencil, a calculator, a record strip for each player, a bag of single digit number cards, a bag of double digit number cards.

❶ Give each player a record strip.

❷ The first player draws one card from the bag of single digit numbers and one from the bag of double digit numbers. Make the biggest three-digit number possible using these two numbers.

So: if you draw 5 and 27, these can be used to make 275 or 527. You choose 527.

❸ Write this number in the first box on your record strip.

❹ Now draw a number card from the bag of double digit numbers and write this number in the second box on your record sheet.

❺ You are now ready to do your calculation.

RECORD SHEET FOR REMAINDERS

SUMMIT

TEACHING CONTENT

★ Practising all four number operations (N: 3c, f; AS: B, C, D; MD: B, C, D)
★ Developing a variety of mental methods of computation with whole numbers up to 100 (N: 3d; AS: B, C, D; MD: B, C, D)
★ Using a calculator to check results (N: 3h, 4c)

PREPARATION

Assembling the game: This game uses one of the full-colour pull-out game boards at the back of the book. To increase durability, mount the game board on to thick card and laminate it. You will also need a bag of two sets of single digit number cards and a bag of two sets of double digit number cards, which can be found on photocopiable pages 34 and 35. Copy directly on to card, or mount on to card after copying, and then cut up to make individual cards.

This game can be played at a variety of levels, so you will need to determine the level of the game for the particular children who are playing it. The game, as described in the 'How to play' sheet, uses both the single digit and the double digit number bags. But you can choose to use only the single digit number bag or only the double digit number bag. Additionally, if you have laminated the game board, you can alter the operations signs by placing sticky labels over them. For instance, if children are not yet ready to tackle the division, you can place labels with one of the other signs over the division signs.

Introducing the game: Having decided on the level of play, discuss the context with the children. What does 'summit' mean? Can they think of other words that mean the same thing? Can they think of other words connected with mountains and mountain climbing? Although the obstacles they will encounter in the game on their 'climb' to the summit are mathematical problems, what sort of problems or obstacles do real mountaineers face?

WHAT YOU NEED

PHOTOCOPIABLE SHEETS
Game board pull-out sheet, 'How to play' sheet 128, number cards sheets 34 and 35.

FOR CONSTRUCTION
Scissors, thick card, glue, clear adhesive plastic, thin card.

FOR PLAYING
Full-colour pull-out game board, 'How to play' sheet, three counters, paper and a pencil for each player, two sets of single digit and two sets of double digit number cards, two bags, a dice and shaker, a calculator.

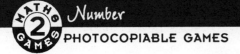

SUMMIT

HOW TO PLAY

This is a game for three players, who should all be working at about the same mathematical level. All players begin on a different START square on the outer (**yellow**) track. In turn, the players throw the dice and move their counter clockwise round the track. More than one player can occupy the same space. When a player lands on a sign square, she takes one card out of the single digit numbers bag and one card out of the double digits numbers bag. She then makes a number sentence using the sign in the middle, for example 17 – 9 = ?. The numbers drawn can be used in any order. She works out the answer mentally, and writes it on a piece of paper. She then checks the solution with the calculator. If it is correct, she puts the number cards back into their respective bags and moves on to a START square on the next track (**red**). If it is wrong, she still puts the number cards back into their bags, but must stay put until her next turn. Play continues with the next player and so on, until someone reaches the summit by solving a problem correctly on the innermost track (**blue**). Players can play on for second and third place.

TEACHER'S ROLE

The level at which this game is played can be determined by the teacher for the particular children playing at any one time. You can choose to use either a single digit or a double digit number bag – or a combination. Although there is an element of chance in the game which might even out the players' levels of ability, the game is best played by children of comparable ability.

During the game, note those aspects of the four operations that cause the most problems. For instance, can the children mentally handle a remainder? (It is expected that division will be the most difficult operation – thus the players start at the furthest point from it, giving them a 'lead in' before they have to tackle its complexities.) How well do they grasp the 'carrying over' of 10 in addition and multiplication? If the children need additional support to use the double digits number bag, let them use pencil and paper to work out their solutions.

HOW TO PLAY SUMMIT

For 3 players.

YOU NEED: the colour game board, 3 counters, paper and a pencil for each player, a bag of two sets of single digit number cards and a bag of two sets of double digit number cards, a dice and shaker, a calculator.

❶ Each player places a counter on a different START square on the outer (**yellow**) track.

❷ In turn, throw the dice and move your counter clockwise round the track. More than one player can occupy the same space.

❸ If you land on a sign square, take one number card out of the single digit numbers bag and one card out of the double digit numbers bag. Make a number sentence with these, using the sign you landed on. The numbers drawn can be used in any order. Work out the answer *in your head* and write it on a piece of paper.

For example, 17 – 9 = ?

❹ Check the solution using the calculator. If it is correct, put the number cards back into their bags and move on to a START square on the next **red** track. If it is wrong, put the number cards back into their bags and stay put until your next turn.

❺ Play continues with the next player and so on, until someone reaches the summit by solving a problem correctly on the **blue** track. Players can play on for 2nd and 3rd place.

ACROBATS

TEACHING CONTENT

★ Developing flexible and effective methods of computation (N: 1a; RTN: D)
★ Using a calculator to explore numbers and processes, including rounding and remainders (N: 1b, 3h; MD: D)
★ Exploring operations upon numbers and their relationships (N: 3c; FE: D)
★ Solving simple equations with missing numbers and symbols (N: 3a; FE: E)

PREPARATION

Assembling the game: This game uses one of the full-colour pull-out game boards at the back of the book. To increase durability, mount the game board on to thick card and laminate it. You will also need a bag of single digit number cards (2 sets of 1 to 9 cards), which can be found on photocopiable page 34. Copy directly on to card, or mount on to card after copying, and then cut up to make individual cards. If you want the players to have their own record strips, cut up the record sheet (photocopiable sheet 132) into individual strips.

Introducing the game: The children should have experience of simple algebraic expressions using symbols (e.g. $n + 4 = 9$, $4 \triangle 5 = 9$) and have been introduced to the idea of using letters instead of numbers. Give some examples to ensure that the children understand what *n* means: I am thinking of a number *n*. It is 4 plus 5. What is *n*? A number *n* is added to 4. The result is 9. What is the number *n*? The children should also be familiar with using a calculator to solve problems involving the four operations, and know how to use the % and √ keys.

HOW TO PLAY

This is a game for two to four players. The object is to climb to the top of the acrobat tower by completing the equation that each acrobat holds with an answer that is within the number range set.

In turn, each player takes out one or two number cards from the single digits bag, according to whether there are one or two digits in the missing number box of the equation she is solving. The first digit drawn represents the ones and the second the tens, so drawing out 1 and then 3 would give 31. The player then solves the equation, using a calculator if required; and if the answer is within the limits given, the player moves her counter on to that acrobat and records the answer on her record strip. The answer she gets for each equation then becomes the *n* number in the next equation. So, if on her first turn a player draws a 1 and 3 as above, she calculates: $100 + 31 = 131$. As this answer is within the limits set for that equation (i.e. between 120 and 150), the player can move her counter on to that acrobat. The number 131 is written on her record strip; on her next turn, that is the number that she will use for the *n* number in the next problem.

At each stage, the answer must be within the limits set. If it is any higher or lower, the player must wait for another turn. Decimal answers are rounded up or down to the nearest whole number. The winner is the

WHAT YOU NEED

PHOTOCOPIABLE SHEETS
'How to play' sheet 131, record sheet 132, number cards sheet 34.

FOR CONSTRUCTION
Scissors, thick card, glue, clear adhesive plastic.

FOR PLAYING
Full-colour pull-out game board, 'How to play' sheet, a counter, record strip and pencil for each player, two sets of 1 to 9 number cards, bag, calculator, scrap paper (optional).

first player to get to the top acrobat. The children can play on until everyone has finished. Then the player with the highest finishing number is the runner-up.

TEACHER'S ROLE

This is a challenging game, and you will need to ensure that the children understand what it is they have to do. Point out that at Step 7, there is no need to draw numbers from the bag to solve the problem. Can they see why? (*Because n is multiplied by itself.*) Observing the game will reveal which children are more confident with the calculator as a tool. During the game, you might encourage the children's mental methods by asking such questions as: Having picked your units digit, what number would be best to pick for the tens digit? How big is the range of numbers your answer must be within? Which of the calculations makes a percentage? Watch how well the children cope with n. You may need to remind them that once the answer from the previous equation is calculated, it is brought up from the level below and becomes the n number for the next equation. Encourage the children to use scrap paper and pencil to jot down their calculations.

HOW TO PLAY ACROBATS

For 2 to 4 players.

YOU NEED: Colour game board, a counter, record strip and pencil for each player, 2 sets of 1 to 9 number cards, bag, calculator, scrap paper (optional).

❶ Choose a column of acrobats and put your counter on the 100.

❷ Take it in turns to climb your column by solving the problem on each acrobat card. At each turn, take out one or two number cards from the single digits bag, according to whether there are one (☐) or two (☐☐) missing numbers in the problem you are solving. The first digit drawn represents the units and the second the tens. So drawing out 1 and then 3 would give 31.

❸ Work out the answer, using a calculator if required. The answer must be between the two numbers underneath the problem. If it is any higher or lower, you must wait for another go.

❹ When you get an answer that fits, move your counter on to that acrobat card and write the answer on your record strip. Return the number cards to the bag for the next player's turn.

❺ When it is your turn again, your last answer becomes the n number in your next problem.

So, if on your first turn you draw 1 and 3, calculate: 100 + 31 = 131. As this answer is within the limits set for that card (i.e between 120 and 150), you can move your counter on to that card and write the number 131 on your record strip. On your next turn, 131 becomes the n number in the problem.

❻ The winner is the first player to get to the top of the column.

❼ Play on until everyone finishes. Then the player with the highest finishing number is the runner-up.

☆ REMEMBER!

If you get a decimal answer, round it up or down to the nearest whole number.

Special section

Number
SPECIAL SECTION

ABOUT THIS SECTION

A problem all teachers face is getting across the concept of place value. One of the greatest leaps in mathematics was the idea that, by placing digits in a particular order, any number could be expressed – certainly an advance over the tally method or Roman numerals. However, the flexibility of our number system also brings with it a certain rigidity. Putting the nought in the wrong position, or placing the digits in the wrong order completely changes the numerical value of a number. So children need to learn that numbers have to be expressed in a set order, and that this extends into the area of decimals.

The resources in this section comprise components for making five different types of number meter, designed to reinforce the child's awareness of place value. In addition to being used for a number of games in this book, they can also be used as general mathematics resources in the classroom. They are simple and inexpensive to make, so each child could have a set of her own to use for all sorts of counting and calculation activities – rather like a ready reckoner or slide rule! The meters with circular wheels add a tactile dimension which appeals to children, but also enable the numbers to go round and round and thus facilitate adding on and taking away.

CONSTRUCTION OF THE METERS

The meter components are best photocopied directly on to the thickest grade of copy card you can get. Alternatively, mount on to card after copying, but make sure that you paste well all over before doing so. Split-pin paper fasteners hold the wheels well enough but, if you can get a card riveter, this is much better. All of the meters except for the Number Meter require internal cut-outs which should be done by the teacher or adult helper with an art knife or sharp scissors. Otherwise, the meters can be made up by most children themselves, and they will enjoy doing so.

You will need to remind children when using the meters that the heads of the paper fasteners are not decimal points. They have no mathematical meaning; they are just there to make the wheels work!

EYE SPY METER

The revolving eyes of the clown enable children to explore numbers between 00 and 99. Try to align the wheels with the tips of the ears so moving the wheels is rather like wiggling the ears! Because the eyes have to be close together, the wheels move in opposite directions (unlike in the other metres) – clockwise for the left eye and anti-clockwise for the right eye.

The game 'Eye spy a big number' on page 26 uses this meter. Other ideas for using this meter are:

Big ten/Little ten
This is a game for a large group with everyone having their own Eye Spy Meter. All eyes are set on 0. Each player in turn has three consecutive throws of the dice and moves the right eye round accordingly. Who has got the biggest right eye number so far? Repeat three consecutive throws for the left eye. Who has got the highest ten number? Who has got the lowest ten number?

Number
SPECIAL SECTION

Double numbers square
This is a game for two using a bag of single digit number cards and one meter. One player has a blue pen; the other a red. On a piece of paper they write the 'double numbers' three on a line starting with 99 88 77 down to 33 22 11. In turn, the players draw a card and move the right eye forward. They keep doing this, adding on in ones and moving both eyes as necessary. As a double number is passed and shows in the clown's eyes, the player passing to or through the number puts a ring round the double number on the paper. Go right through to 99. The player with the most rings in the double number square wins.

Lucky numbers
This is a class game with children selecting their numbers in spare moments. Write down six numbers between 1 and 54 but don't let the children see. Each child then uses the Eye Spy Meter and a bag of single digit number cards to create six numbers. This is done by taking a card out of the bag and advancing the units wheel that number of times. This gives the first number which is written down. The card is replaced in the bag and a second card drawn. Advance the wheel (or wheels if over ten), note this second number, and so on until six numbers have been created. When everyone has had a go, let them compare their numbers with the ones you wrote down. Who has got the most lucky numbers?

MONEY METER

Usually children's first introduction to decimals is through money. They will see decimal prices in stores and so will be familiar with the notation, if not the actual concept of whole pounds with pence as decimal parts of a pound. The Money Meter should help to make the concept clear. It is best to colour the two decimal wheels red so that they are distinguished from the whole numbers. The coins and notes on the face of the meter indicate the relative values as well as the 'tenths' and 'hundredths'.

The games 'Maker a fiver' on page 45 and 'Coin hopscotch' on page 48 use this meter. Other ideas for using this meter are:

£1.88
Any number of children can play so long as each has a Money Meter of her own. A bag of coin cards is needed. Each round, the players take a coin card and put it back in the bag. To move their meters, the cards have to be drawn in order of smallest to biggest. So 1p has to be drawn before progressing to 2p and then 5p, 10p, 20p, 50p and finally £1. Any other card drawn means wait until the next round. The players move their meters adding on the coins. They should pass through this sequence: £0.01 (1p), £0.03 (2p), £0.08 (5p), £0.18 (10p), £0.38 (20p), £0.88 (50p) and £1.88 (£1). The first to get this number wins.

Sale price
This game sets off with £9.99 on the Money Meter. There can be any number of players. Throw a dice and subtract it from the right-hand pence wheel. The second throw is deducted from the second wheel and the third from the pounds. Make a note of the number. When everyone has finished see who has got the biggest sale price reduction, that is, who has the smallest amount.

Multiple money
Again any number of children can play this game. A throw of the dice determines how far each wheel is to be turned. There are six rounds. The

first round determines how many 1p coins the player can turn on the pence wheel. So if 5 is thrown, the wheel is turned to £0.05. The second dice throw gives the number of 2p coins which are added on to the existing number. So if 4 is thrown this is 4 × 2p allowing 8p to be added on the pence wheels giving £0.13. The game continues in this fashion for 5p, 10p, 20p and 50p. The largest total wins.

DECIMAL METER

This is similar to the Money Meter and uses the same number wheels. However, the drawings on the face of the meter do illustrate the decimal value of each number. Whereas the child using the Money Meter could get by relating the numbers to the coins, there is no such prop here. However, the three forms of the decimal fractions are shown to make understanding them a bit easier.

The game 'Skyline' on page 77 uses this meter. Other ideas for using this meter are:

Biggest number
Any number can play. Use a bag of single digit number cards to pick cards for each wheel. The first determines the number of hundredths, the second the number of tenths and the third the whole numbers. When everyone has a number, discuss who has got the biggest. See which numbers the children think are biggest – Is 8.00 bigger than 6.97?

Three to win
This is a game for a small group. Each player should have a Decimal Meter. To emphasise the fraction equivalent of the decimals, a three-sided equilateral spinner is used, one side marked 1/100, one 1/10 and the other 1. It is used with a dice. Each player takes it in turn to spin the spinner and then roll the dice. If the spinner shows 1/100 and the dice 5, the player moves the hundredths wheel five places giving 0.05. The next round's number has to be entered in an empty box. So, in the example, the player needs a 1 or 1/10. Getting another 1/100 is a wasted effort. The first player to get a number in all three boxes wins. Play goes on until everyone has finished. Then ask the players to read out their numbers and question them along the following lines: How many hundredths have you got? What does the 3 stand for in your number?

9.99
This is a game for two or more players. Use the three-sided fraction spinner described above and a dice. Each player needs a Decimal Meter. Set the meters at 9.99. Play in rounds, spinning the spinner to give which box is being used and then throwing the dice to give a number to be subtracted from 9.99. There will be times when the number to be subtracted is bigger than the number in the box. In this case no move can be made and play passes on to the next player. Once 0 has been entered in a box, it cannot be changed. The first player to get three noughts wins.

NOUGHTY METER

This meter uses strips rather than wheels to represent the numbers, as its purpose is to emphasise the relative values of nought. By combining it with the four operational processes, it allows the child to investigate what happens when numbers ending in noughts are added, subtracted,

Number
SPECIAL SECTION

multiplied and divided. It leads on to the short cuts of adding or subtracting noughts from the end when multiplying or dividing.

The game 'Noughty' on page 73 uses this meter. Other ideas for using this meter are:

Biggest/smallest number

This is a game for a large group using a bag of single digit number cards. Each child takes two cards from the bag. Start with the add sign and see who can make the biggest sum. Who has made the smallest sum? Both are winners. Change the sign to subtract but keep the same cards, which can be changed around but not replaced. Again, who has the biggest or the smallest number? Do the same for multiply and divide.

4 noughts

This is for 2 or more players. Set the sign on multiplication. Use a bag of single digit number cards and draw out two numbers. They can be used in any way to make a product with 4 noughts in it. The combinations will be pairings like $500 \times 20 = 10\,000$, $800 \times 50 = 40\,000$. Keep playing until someone does so and wins.

Nearest 1

Whereas the object of the previous game was to finish with a number with as many noughts as possible, this game, for any number of players, has the reverse objective. Set the sign on division. Using a bag of single digit number cards, players juggle two chosen numbers to make a number sentence with the answer as near 1 as possible. Let the children try to work out the answer themselves, then check using a calculator. To make it easier, decimals can be ignored.

NUMBER METER

This works rather like the old-fashioned gas meter and demonstrates numbers between 0000 and 9999. It can be altered to suit any number ranging between these limits. For example, delete the thousands and the meter shows hundreds, tens and units.

The games 'What's the difference?' on page 69 and 'Number roulette' on page 112 use this meter. Other ideas for using this meter are:

Thousands

This is a game to find who can get the most thousands. Each player selects a card from a bag of single digit number cards. This is the units number and the 'units' wheel is turned to show it. The card is returned and a second card is taken for the tens, another for the hundreds and a fourth for the thousands. This gives a four-figure number. Who has the highest?

9999

This is a game for any number of players playing one at a time. Each player sets 9999 on the meter and then throws a dice in sequence. First throw is subtracted from the 9 thousands, second throw from the 9 hundreds, the third throw from the tens and the fourth from the units. Who has got the biggest number? He or she wins. For a change, the winner could be the player with the smallest number.

Mirror numbers

Any number of players can play this game. The wheels are set according to four throws of a dice – first throw units, second tens, third hundreds and fourth thousands. Jot down the number. Now reverse the number. If it was 3251, it becomes 1523. What is the difference between them? Use a calculator if you like. The smallest difference wins.

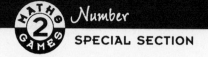

EYE SPY METER CLOWN FACE

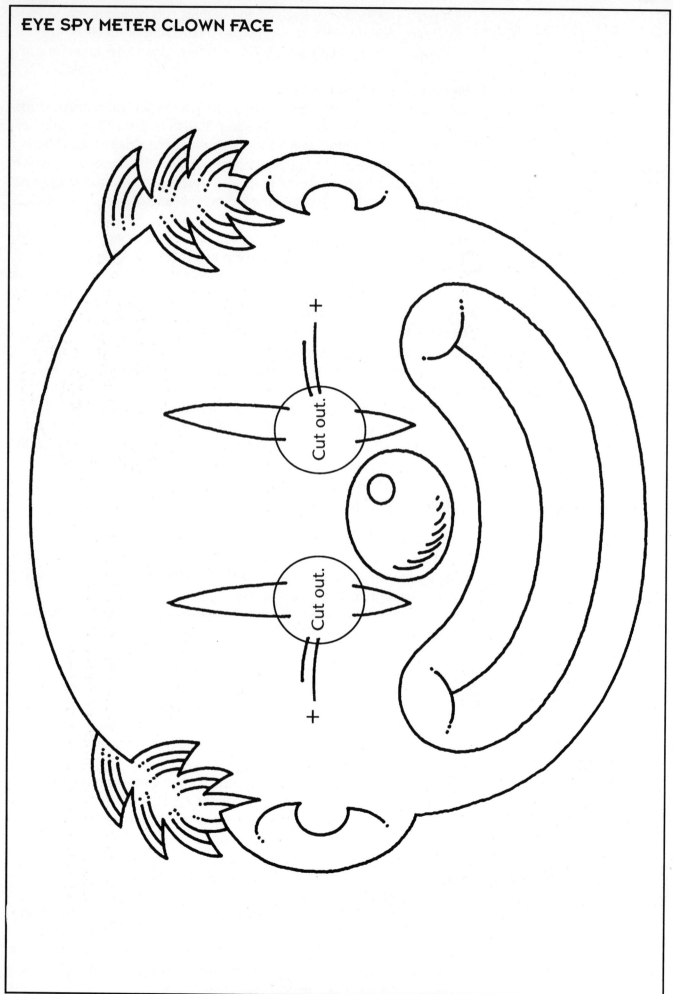

EYE SPY METER NUMBER WHEELS

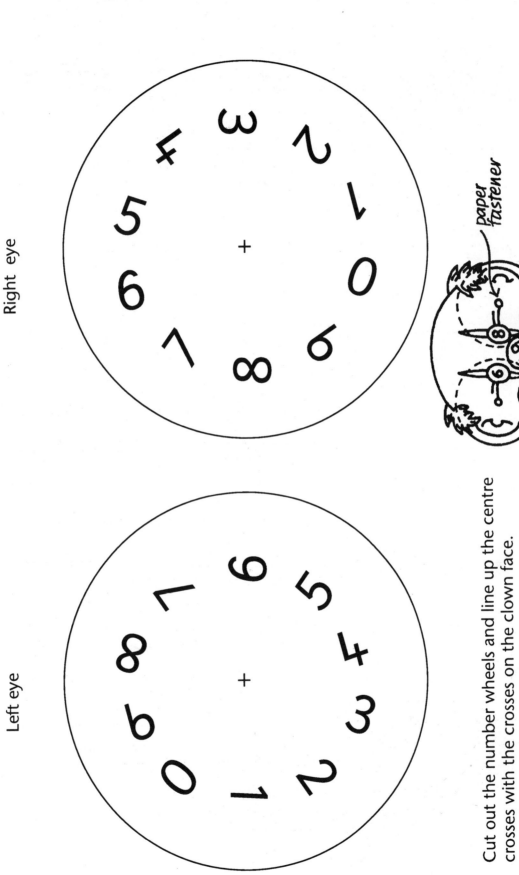

Right eye

Left eye

Cut out the number wheels and line up the centre crosses with the crosses on the clown face. Fix with paper fasteners as shown.

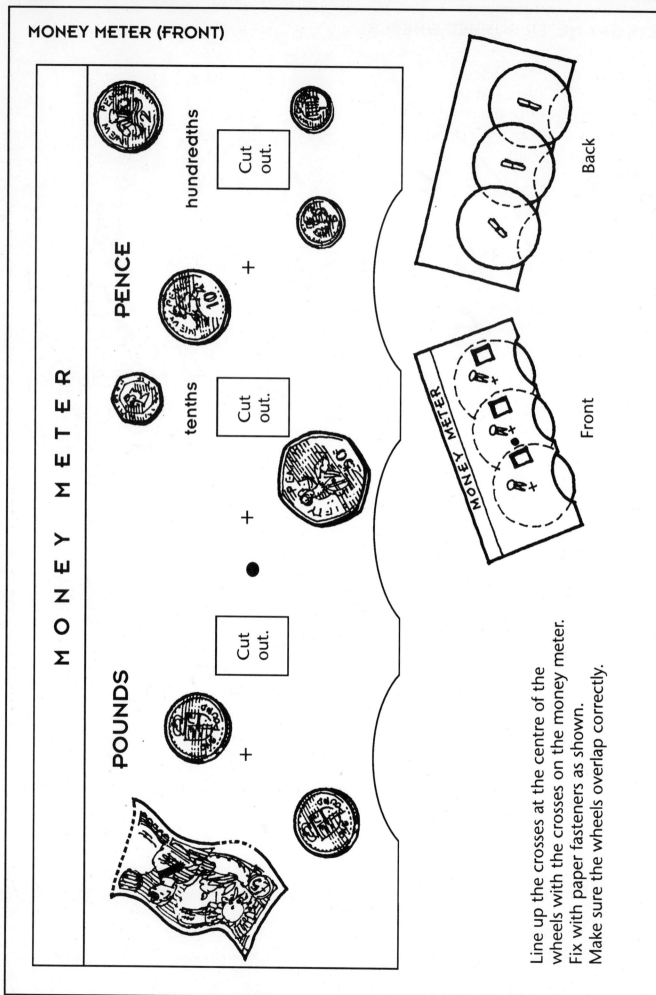

MONEY METER/DECIMAL METER NUMBER WHEELS

Cut out the number wheels. Colour 2 wheels red and use these to the right of the decimal point. This will help distinguish these numbers from whole numbers.

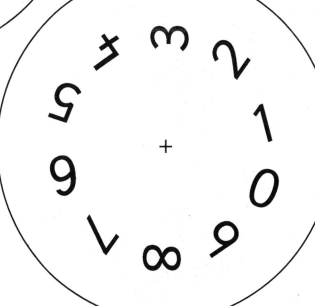

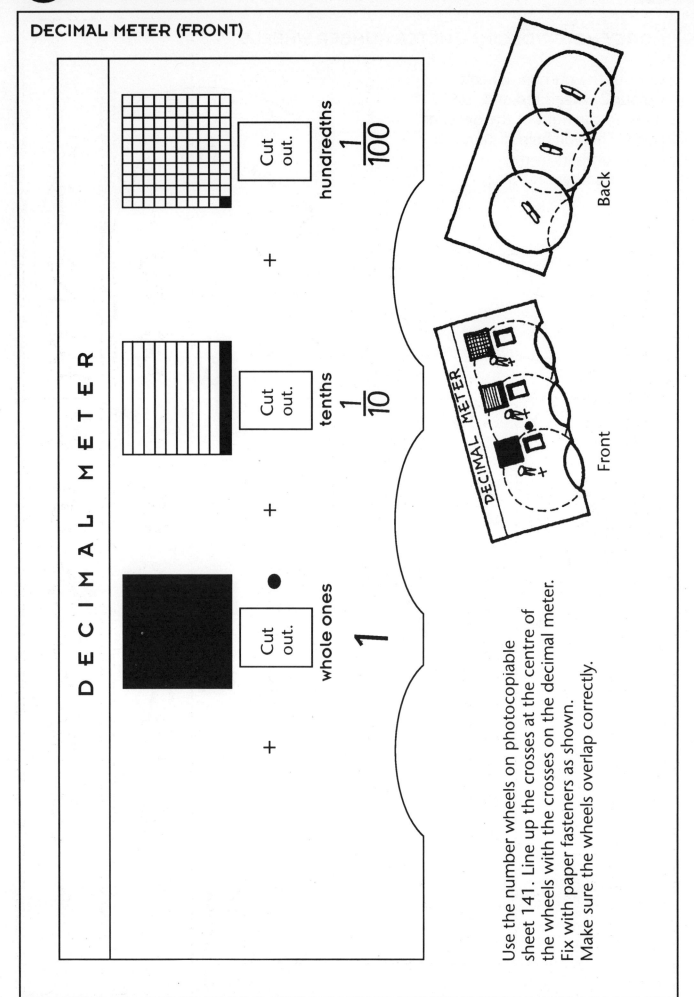

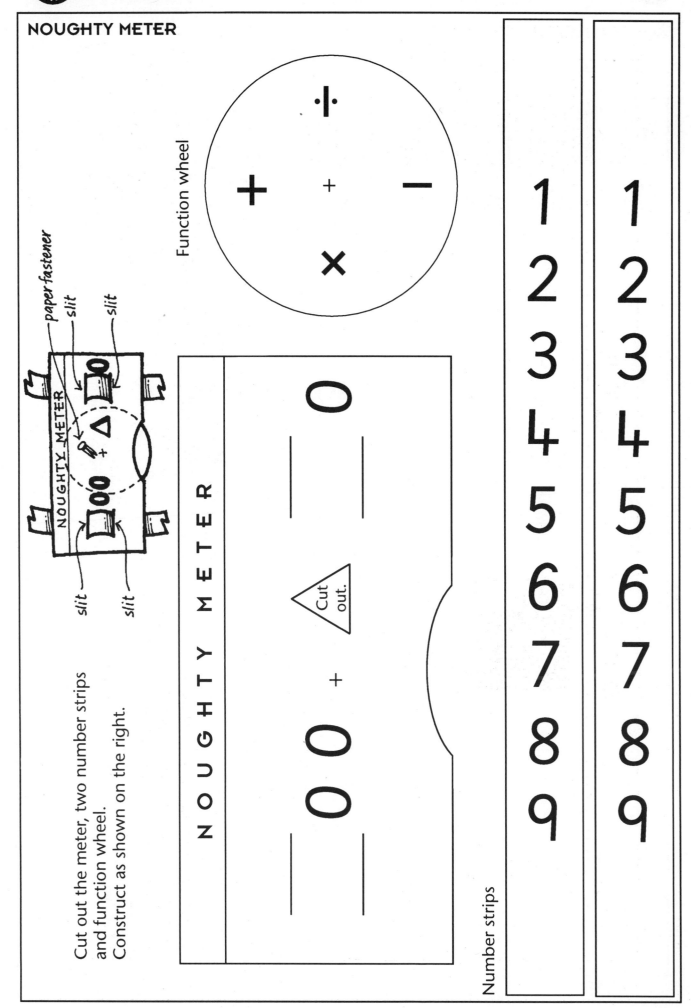

NUMBER METER

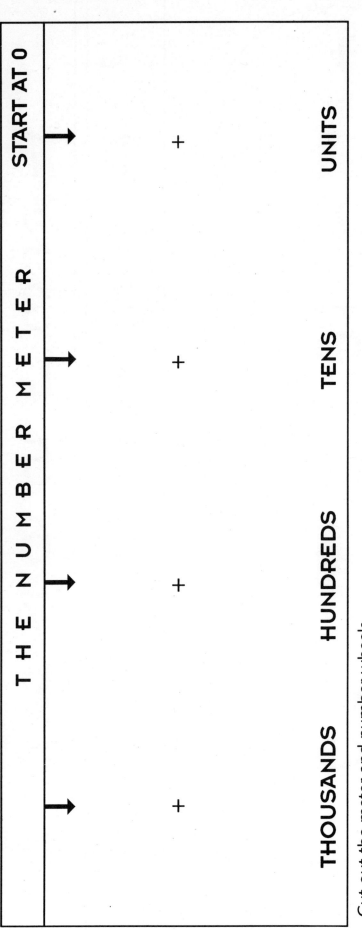

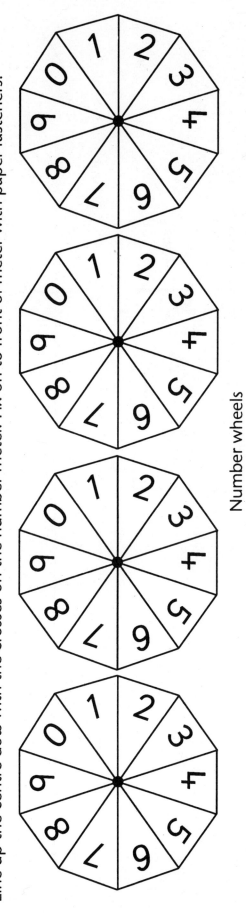

Number wheels

Cut out the meter and number wheels.
Line up the centre dots with the crosses on the number meter. Fix on to front of meter with paper fasteners.